D1590055

Otto a Davis

Rebellion

and

Authority

Rebellion and Authority

An Analytic Essay on Insurgent Conflicts

Nathan Leites and Charles Wolf, Jr.

The RAND Corporation

Markham Series in Public Policy Analysis

MARKHAM PUBLISHING COMPANY

Chicago

MARKHAM SERIES IN PUBLIC POLICY ANALYSIS

Julius Margolis and Aaron Wildavsky, Editors

Bogart, ed., *Social Research and the Desegregation of the U.S. Army*

Davis and Dolbeare, *Little Groups of Neighbors: The Selective Service System*

Feldstein, *Economic Analysis for Health Service Efficiency*

Hansen and Weisbrod, *Benefits, Costs, and Finance of Public Higher Education*

Leites and Wolf, *Rebellion and Authority: An Analytic Essay on Insurgent Conflicts*

PREFACE

As a subject for analysis, Rebellion and Authority is richly—perhaps prodigally—endowed with historical experience and empirical detail. It is also a subject whose wealth of detail is accompanied by a poverty of theory. In this respect, the study of insurgent conflict—conflict between authorities and rebellions—contrasts sharply with the study of strategic nuclear conflict, in which the theory is better developed and experience is, fortunately, lacking.

The primary aim of this book is generalization and theory—to develop and illustrate a way of analyzing insurgent conflicts—rather than application of the analytical method to actual conflicts. The authors' attention is concentrated principally on less developed countries, but occasionally we also try to suggest how various points can be applied to urban and campus rebellions in the more developed countries. The pattern of argument is to advance hypotheses and illustrate (rather than test) them by reference to a number of specific cases. Hence, the two contrasting terms in the subtitle: "analytic" and "essay"—one referring to an aspiration toward rigor, the other to the limited nature of that effort as well as to the defects of the data used. The authors are principally concerned, as noted, with moving the discussion of insurgent conflict toward the level that has been attained in the better discussions of nuclear conflict.

Hence, more attention is given to establishing the categories (variables) and functional relationships that need to be examined than to specifying the precise weights to be attached to them. Indeed, the precise weights that should be attached to *demand* and *supply* considerations in the growth of rebellions, or to profit-maximizing and damage-limiting factors (as distinct from political and nonmaterial factors) in influencing population preferences between the contesting sides, cannot be specified without a much more detailed study of particular insurgencies than has been attempted in this essay.

Moreover, the authors themselves hold divergent views on the proper weights to be assigned to different factors—in general and in several specific cases, although both would agree that comprehensive studies of particular cases might well remove these divergences. While neither believes that popular preferences are unimportant in their influence on outcomes, they perhaps differ as to the relative importance of such factors. One author (Wolf) places somewhat greater stress on supply (efficiency) considerations than on demand (preference) considerations. The other author (Leites) conjectures that demand considerations (and within demand, political and nonmaterial rather than material considerations) are sources of influence of the same magnitude as the supply considerations.

The authors also have divergent views on the war in Vietnam, which has been a compelling influence on their thinking throughout the several years of collaboration on this book. Although both have had serious disagreements with U.S. policies in Vietnam, the principal disagreement of one concerns the efficiency with which these policies have been conducted, and that of the other, the moral acceptability of these policies even if conducted efficiently. Hence, this divergence is closely associated with that mentioned previously.°

For those who may wish to associate authors, divergences, and chapters, the burden of Chapters 1, 3, 5, and 7 is Wolf's; of Chapter 6, Leites'. Chapters 2, 4, and 8 are joint products. While neither author fully endorses all of the book, both endorse most of it, and, of course at least one of us endorses each part of it. Both authors fully endorse the analytical approach of the book as a whole.

At various places in the book, we have tried to consider the distinct viewpoints of the rebellion, or the authority, or both, as well as the viewpoints of outside parties aiding one or the other. If we are successful in the balance sought, a hypothetical seminar,

°For some aspects of the authors' views on this war, see Nathan Leites, **The Viet Cong Style of Politics,** The RAND Corporation, RM-5487-1, May, 1969, Santa Monica, and Charles Wolf, Jr., "Vietnam Prospects and Precepts," **Asian Survey,** March 1969, pp. 157-162.

consisting of (1) Giap and Magsaysay as representatives of rebellions and authorities, respectively (although Giap could fit in both categories and, as a matter of less well-known fact, so could Magsaysay), and (2) T. E. Lawrence and Edward Lansdale as their respective advisors, should find substantial and roughly equal agreement with propositions advanced in the book. We think they would.

Nevertheless, at times and in particular chapters, the balance may lapse. Sometimes the posture of the authority and, specifically, of U.S. policy in relation to authority, is adopted more completely than perfect balance would warrant. This should be avoided, among other reasons, because more effective policy on *either* side depends itself on clearer analysis and understanding of *both* sides. Moreover, authorities are not invariably worthy of support by those inside or outside the country; nor are rebellions; nor neutrals. No invariant judgment is possible on this matter, and none is implied in the book. In any event, the balance between viewpoints is surely more even if the book is looked at as a whole, as the authors hope it will be, rather than chapter by chapter.

During several years of work on this study, the authors have benefited from oral and written comments—frequently critical—by a number of people at RAND and other institutions, in particular Daniel Ellsberg, Fred Iklé, Martin Lipset, Andrew Marshall, Lucian Pye, James Schlesinger, Brigadier Ted Serong, Francis West, and Albert and Roberta Wohlstetter. Since it has been pointed out earlier that the authors themselves retain, indeed relish, various disagreements with each other, it goes without saying that inclusion on this list in no sense implies agreement with what is said in the book. We wish to acknowledge the support given this work by The RAND Corporation under its program of research for the Advanced Research Projects Agency of the Department of Defense. None of these organizations, any more than the previously listed people, necessarily endorses any of the viewpoints expressed by the authors. We also want to acknowledge the editorial assistance of Malcolm Palmatier, and the research and bibliographical help of Valentina Laffin.

Nathan Leites
Charles Wolf, Jr.

CONTENTS

5   THE AUTHORITY'S VIEWPOINT: CONCEPTS AND CONDUCT OF COUNTERREBELLION   71

6   INFLICTING DAMAGE   90

Chapter 1

INTRODUCTION

In almost every year since World War II at least one insurgency has been underway in the less developed areas—Greece, Burma, Malaya, the Philippines, Vietnam, Kenya, Laos, the Congo, Algeria, Cuba, the Dominican Republic, Yemen, and Thailand. (The chronological listing conceals wide differences in scope, intensity, and duration, as well as some other interesting and usually unrecognized points. For example, an insurgency can be maintained at low intensity over a long time, indeed in the case of Burma almost throughout the post-World War II period. And an insurgency that has been severely abridged, if not totally broken in the past can start again, as in the Philippines and South Vietnam.)

One can think of reasons for expecting this high frequency to diminish in years to come: for example, the lessons learned from Vietnam by both internal and external participants; and the termination of alien rule in most of the world.[1] One can also think of reasons for expecting the frequency to remain the same or increase: for example, opposite lessons learned from Vietnam (the lessons are, in other words, ambiguous, and various inferences can be drawn from them); the persistence of deep frictions, inequities, and grievances in the less developed countries; and the heightened frustration that is likely to accompany unconstrained promises and constrained efforts to produce remedies. In sum, the reasons for expecting this frequency to diminish

[1] For a statement of such reasons, see Paul Kecskemeti, **Insurgency as a Strategic Problem**, The RAND Corporation, RM-5160-PR, February, 1967, Santa Monica, Calif.

are not obviously stronger than the reasons for expecting it to remain the same or increase.

Each major insurgency is, in some sense, unique, as suggested by the diversity of areas and circumstances in the list. But most of them have shared many features—organization, tactics, violence, coercion, persuasion, ideology, internal grievance, external influence. The common features make insurgency a proper subject for more general analysis. The diversity warrants caution to avoid pushing generalizations too far.

What are the sources and causes of insurgency? How are they combined and converted into an effective insurgent organization and operation? What concepts and doctrines can help in understanding it, from the side of either the initiator or the opponent? How can an insurgency be made to wax and win, or wane and wilt? What programs can be formulated to propitiate insurgency or deter it, or control or suppress it once it has started? These are the questions with which this book is principally concerned. Our aim is to suggest answers, and illustrate them by referring to specific insurgencies as well as to the use of organized violence in noninsurgency contexts. In some cases, we shall refer also to similarities and differences between recent insurgencies in the less developed countries (LDCs) and contemporary urban disorders and campus rebellions in the more developed countries (MDCs). Much of the analytical framework can be applied as well to the latter contingencies, although we shall only try to do this to a limited extent.

Insurgency, or *rebellion* as we shall call it, is a subject that is especially difficult for Americans to view with dispassion. Americans' views of themselves and their national traditions tend to involve them, indeed in many cases to commit them, to the insurgent side. We are, or conceive ourselves to be, an insurgent people originating in a tradition of rebellion against inequitable, onerous, and illegitimate authority. As one senator, usually not given to exaggerated rhetoric, put it in commenting on the supposed incongruity of the U.S. role in Vietnam: "We came into being through a revolution, through insurgency . . . [and we have] sympathetically responded to moves of independence [elsewhere]."[2]

---

[2] **Congressional Record**, United States Senate, February 16, 1966, p. 3020.

This Jeffersonian heritage is reflected in a contemporary disposition to embrace the symbols and slogans of "popular" uprisings, and to feel uncomfortable and self-doubting if we do not. We sometimes identify with Robin Hood and the Minutemen (eighteenth century, not twentieth), and reject the Sheriff of Nottingham and the Redcoats—and we tend emotionally to transmute the complex greys of contemporary insurgencies into the purer whites and blacks of history and legend.

The American attitude of sympathy and attachment toward an insurgent cause is not inconsistent with a readiness to react, even overreact, with massive military force against those insurgencies we have wittingly or unwittingly become committed to oppose for reasons of supposedly realistic international politics. A disposition to overreact can be traced in part to the frustration and anguish that result from having to oppose an adversary we might, by heritage, prefer to support.

The combination of a Jeffersonian heritage with contemporary international politics disposes us to oscillate between sympathy and identification with an insurgency on the one hand and impassioned and self-righteous hostility on the other. Either attitude impedes cool (let alone cold) analysis, as well as prudent choices of when and how to oppose, support, or ignore an insurgency. The view taken in this book is that such choices, from the standpoint of U.S. interests, are neither obvious nor invariable. To make better choices requires an improved understanding of insurgency in general, and of particular insurgencies at particular times and places.

A study of insurgency and counterinsurgency might appropriately begin by considering the words themselves. Both terms have been used so loosely that their meaning is unclear and frequently strong feelings are evoked by them despite, or because of, their ambiguity. In much of the underdeveloped world the term insurgent more often denotes the "good guys" than the "bad guys." (In Mexico City, for example, a main boulevard is the *Avenida de los Insurgentes*.)

For these reasons we shall use instead two terms that are probably more accurate, surely fresher, and perhaps less partisan: *rebellion* and *authority*. The dictionary defines rebellion as "open, *organized*, and often *armed*, resistance," whereas insurgency is defined as a revolt "*not reaching the proportions of an organized revolution"* [emphasis added]. Since it is precisely the organizational aspects that are central to its strength as well as to its analysis, rebellion is a more useful term.

Authority is a legal and legitimized right and capacity to command. Of course, authority can be employed for good or bad purposes, and for purposes that are congenial, hostile, or indifferent to American or other interests. These purposes should be of first importance in policy formulation—that is, in the choice of whether and how to support, oppose, or remain neutral toward a particular authority structure—but they are not the primary concern of this study. In principle, the analysis of what makes rebellion succeed or fail can be used by those interested in its success or those interested in its failure. In deterring or fighting rebellions, or in helping them emerge and advance toward victory, what needs to be made central to the discussion is the structure of authority—how to strengthen and maintain it on the one hand, or how to undermine, destroy, and supplant it on the other. This book is an attempt to identify and assess the characteristics and operational modes of rebellion and authority under conditions of stress.

Toward this end, Chapters 2 and 3 consider theoretical approaches to the problem of rebellion and authority. Chapter 2 examines the pervasive view that insurgent conflict, unlike other conflicts—or to a greater extent—is a struggle for the *hearts and minds* of the people, a *political rather than military conflict.* Chapter 3 elaborates an alternative approach that views an emerging rebellion as a system and an organizational technique, and views the process of countering a rebellion in terms of weakening its organization while strengthening the structure of authority. The remaining chapters are concerned with applications of this approach.

Specifically, Chapter 4 considers the structure and operations of the R system (we shall use the letter R hereinafter to stand for rebellion or insurgency, and the letter A to refer to authority). Chapter 4 looks at R from the rebellion's point of view. The aim is to set forth various propositions concerning the proclivities and operational characteristics of R: what R*s* typically do, and what seems efficient for R*s* to do, under different circumstances.

Chapter 5 examines the process by which an authority does

(or should) conduct counterrebellion. It looks at A from the authority's point of view. Again, it aims to suggest what A*s* typically do, and to advance several propositions concerning what seems efficient for A*s* to do, in this kind of war, in contrast to other forms of conflict in which authority is threatened from without rather than from within.

Chapter 6 reviews the use of coercion by both R and A, and considers when and how it may be efficient to threaten or impose damage on a target for the purpose of influencing its behavior, and when it may be efficient to refrain from or limit damage.

Chapter 7 inspects the role of intelligence and information in this type of conflict as compared with others. It is concerned with the theory of intelligence in insurgent conflicts—in particular, the tradeoffs among intelligence, firepower, and mobility at different stages of insurgency—and with efficient techniques for obtaining and using intelligence.

Finally, Chapter 8 summarizes the principal conclusions and draws inferences for policy and further research.

Chapter 2

CURRENT BELIEFS
AND THEORY

A widely held theory about R contends that popular attitudes, sympathy, and support play the decisive role in enabling R to get started, gain momentum, and erupt into "liberation wars." International politics, external assistance, governmental efficiency, and military factors are also acknowledged to play a role; but their influence is supposedly subsidiary, not merely in a few cases but in most or all of them. According to this theory, the primary activating force behind R lies in popular likes and dislikes; the erosion of public sympathy and support for established institutions; and the acquisition of such sympathy and support by R. In the same manner, the theory contends that for counterinsurgency to be successful, support must be recaptured by A.

Contentions of this sort take many forms and intensities. Certain key phrases reflect the mood of the theory. They include the familiar assertion that insurgency and counterinsurgency represent a struggle for the hearts and minds of the people, rather than a struggle for territory or against military forces.[1] Another assertion holds that counterinsurgency is a political, social, and economic, rather than a military problem.[2] A third

[1] See statement by President Marcos of the Philippines, New York Times, September 16, 1966; also, Roger Hilsman's statement before the Senate Subcommittee To Investigate Problems Connected with Refugees and Escapees, United States Senate, Refugee Problems in South Vietnam and Laos, Washington, U.S. Government Printing Office, 1965, p. 318 ff.

[2] Charles Wolf, Jr., U.S. Policy and the Third World (Boston: Little, Brown, 1967), Chapter 3; George K. Tanham, Communist Revolutionary Warfare: The Vietminh in Indochina (New York: Praeger, 1961), pp. 76-77 ff.

takes the form of Mao Tse-tung's image of the insurgents as "the fish in the sea," with the populace comprising the environment that incubates, nourishes, and sustains R. Communist doctrine proclaims loudly and clearly the primacy of popular afflictions and affections in permitting and precipitating "wars of national liberation." The preferred communist view depicts R as mainly indigenous, voluntary, and nationalistic. Eruption comes principally from the accumulation of internal grievances and afflictions, resulting from an exploitative, antiquated traditional or colonial past.[3]

However, while communist doctrine stresses internal sentiments and the hearts and minds of large masses of people, the point should not be overdrawn. The doctrine is sufficiently comprehensive and flexible to recognize also the importance of internal organization, leadership, and guidance of mass sentiments, and external support for these organizational efforts. The counterpoise of emphasis between internal and external efforts, voluntarism and coercion, and individual sentiments and organizational strength is pervasive.[4] It is neatly reflected in Mao's well-known contradictory propositions: on the one hand, "weapons are an important factor in war but not the decisive one; it is man and not material that counts"; while, on the other hand, "political power grows out of the barrel of a gun."[5]

The counterpoise is indeed more in evidence in communist writings and doctrine than in some of the influential American writings and opinions to which we now turn. Without attempting a detailed exposition, we shall discuss briefly some of the major

[3] Mao Tse-tung, **Selected Works,** Vol. II (New York: International Publishers, 1954), 13-18; Vo Nguyen Giap, **People's War, People's Army** (New York: Praeger, 1962), pp. 12, 25 ff.; Truong Chinh, **Primer For Revolt** (New York: Praeger, 1963), pp. 59-67 ff.); Che Guevara, **On Guerrilla Warfare** (New York: Praeger, 1961), pp. 3-10, 30-32, 70-85.

[4] Consider Giap's 1965 speech recognizing the major role of external support from the Democratic Republic of (North) Vietnam in obtaining a "people's victory" in South Vietnam, in contrast to Lin Piao's depreciation of the importance of external assistance to the Viet Cong, in his speech of September, 1965. And Mao, while on the one hand stressing the importance of internal, popular support, also notes that:

[It] is a mistaken idea . . . [that] victory is possible . . . without international help. In the epoch in which imperialism exists, it is impossible to win victory in any country without various forms of help from the international revolutionary forces. Mao Tse-tung, **op. cit.,** Vol. V, 416.

[5] Mao Tse-tung, **op. cit.,** Vol. II, 192, 272.

propositions characterizing the prevalent views in the United States and elsewhere on insurgency and counterinsurgency, together with some evidence that casts doubt on the validity of these propositions.[6]

Proposition 1: R requires popular support to get started and gain momentum, and guerrilla forces require popular support to conduct successful military operations. (Conversely, acquiring popular support by A is essential if operations against R are to be successful.)

Both the interest and validity of this proposition depend crucially on the meaning ascribed to "popular support." If the term refers merely to conduct on the part of some segment of the population that is tolerant of R (in the sense that it permits R to exist) then the proposition is a truism: for R to exist, the behavior of the population must permit R to exist.

If, to take another possible interpretation, the proposition means that R's prospects are improved by *some* acts by *some* part [7] of the population which positively benefit R (for example providing food, recruits, information, and the like), then the proposition is both nontruistic and defensible. But these merits are purchased at a price that is high for the usual hearts-and-minds view of the problem. The strength of the original proposition is considerably reduced, and the *motives*—whether preferences (sympathies) of the population, a desire for profit, or a fear of damage—underlying these *limited* acts by *limited* numbers of the populace are left unspecified. This second interpretation of the proposition is closely linked with an alternative

---

[6] Although we shall avoid detailed citations, the views to be described can be generously documented from various official, academic, and journalistic sources. See, for example, Robert McNamara's address to the American Society of Newspaper Editors in Montreal on May 18, 1966, Department of Defense Release No. 422-66; William J. Fulbright, **The Arrogance of Power** (New York: Random House, 1966), pp. 69-81 ff.; Roger Hilsman, **To Move a Nation** (Garden City: Doubleday, 1967), pp. 424-431 ff.; David Halberstam, **The Making of a Quagmire** (New York: Random House, 1964), Chapter 7; and Chalmers Johnson, "Civilian Loyalties and Guerrilla Conflict," **World Politics,** Vol. XIV, No. 4, July, 1962, 646-661.

The hearts-and-minds view is not confined to the United States. It is widespread in Western Europe and Japan, for example, as well as in the more developed parts of Latin America. Indeed, perhaps the only places where this view is distinctly in the minority are countries where communist insurgencies have been successfully countered—for example, Korea, Greece, and Malaysia.

[7] And perhaps an extremely small part. See pp. 9-10 for some rough estimates.

approach to analyzing insurgency which we favor and will discuss later.[8]

If, at the other end of the spectrum of meanings, the proposition is intended to suggest that the existence and growth of R require (and reflect) the preferential ardor of a large part (for example, 25 percent, 51 percent, or 75 percent) of the population, then the proposition loses in defensibility more than it gains in importance.

This interpretation of the proposition is vulnerable on the following grounds: (1) its implication concerning the scope of actions required by R from the population, (2) the proportion of the population required to engage in these acts, and (3) the ascription to these actors of motives of preference and sympathy.

Concerning the first two grounds, those acts that directly provide the essential material and human inputs required for the existence and growth of R need only engage a small fraction of the population. This assertion applies in the middle stages of insurgency as well as in the embryonic stages. Of course, the proportion of the population whose support is required by R will vary with its stage, scale, and activity as well as with the criterion used to define "support." Furthermore, R's growth may be eased by having a larger fraction of the population behind it in some localities, even though it receives support from a very small fraction of the population as a whole. According to some estimates, the fraction of the total population providing *active* support for the Malayan rebels in 1951 and the Viet Cong as late as 1964 was about one percent, although the percentage was higher within particular local areas.[9] Similarly, the costs of recruiting, training, and maintaining guerrilla forces of the size that were active in Malaya and Vietnam during these periods were not large. For example, according to an unpublished RAND study based on data derived from interviews with former mem-

---

[8] See Chapter 3.

[9] The fractions cited assume 10,000 guerrilla units actively supported by 50,000 backup people in Malaya in 1951; and 35,000 and 100,000, respectively, in Vietnam in 1964. Cf. Sir Robert Thompson, **Defeating Communist Insurgency: Experiences from Malaya and Vietnam** (London: Chatto & Windus, 1966), pp. 47-48. Thompson uses the term "active positive supporters" to describe those persons providing direct support outside the guerrilla units.

bers of the Viet Cong, food consumption by a Viet Cong battalion in one province in 1963 was less than one percent of available food supplies in the VC-controlled area of the province.

The only "act" that R needs desperately from a large proportion of the populace is *nondenunciation* (that is, eschewing the act of informing against R) and noncombat against it. It is in this sense that one might interpret Guevara's use of the term popular support to differentiate robber bands from guerrilla bands:

> . . . robber bands . . . possess all the characteristics of a guerrilla band . . . They lack only one thing: the support of the people. And, inevitably, these bands are caught. . . .[10]

Robber bands are more easily and safely denunciable than are insurgents, because robber bands typically (though not always) lack the memory and the follow-up that makes denunciation of R unattractive.

The rebels' need not to be denounced by the population may be satisfied in some cases because the population is largely in sympathy with them. But it can also be satisfied because the people want to avoid R's sanctions; or because the people, while they lack sympathy for R or even dislike it, also dislike A or do not feel so strongly in favor of A as to denounce R. For the crucial matter of pervasive nondenunciation, R must carefully scrutinize not how much ardor R itself commands, but rather how much favor A commands. Conversely, A must rely on the fervor of part of a probably random, if not adversely biased, sample of the populace that happens to have acquired information about R so that denunciation would be effective. In the environment of underdeveloped societies, with their conflicts and afflictions, whose governments' capacity to provide remedies is severely limited even when their intention is not (and often it is), the outcome of this asymmetrical contest is not encouraging to A. The best it can do is likely to fall short of commanding that degree of fervor from the population which would result in denunciation of, and active resistance to, R.[11]

[10] Che Guevara, **op. cit.,** pp. 6-7.

[11] Cf. Wolf, **op. cit.,** Chapter 3; see also Chapter 3, below, for further discussion on this point.

Finally, the proposition concerning popular support is vulnerable in ascribing acts that support R—including, but not confined to, nondenunciation—to the preferences of the population rather than to other motives. To start with, R does require a core—but only an extremely small one—of fervent supporters whose preferences are pure and in a sense total. (More precisely, they prefer paying an infinite price, death, to accepting the perpetuation of A.) But as R grows, it relies increasingly on acts of support from segments of the populace whose preferences are much more flexible. (For example, where there is a market for the services and commodities that R requires, provision of such support need imply no preference for R whatsoever; the producing units in the population simply sell the inputs that R needs, at market prices.)[12] The behavior of these segments may be motivated in large part by fear and advantage, combined with predictions of the conflict's outcome. We shall call behavior based on fear of the consequences of acting otherwise *damage-limiting*, and behavior based on considerations of gain *profit-maximizing*. In both cases, behavior can be critically influenced by expectations (forecasts, predictions) of how the conflict between A and R will eventually be resolved.[13]

Such motives and influences may generate most of the actions that R's growth and success require. It is therefore erroneous to ascribe these actions to "pure preferences" on the part of the population. The degree of preference for (or resistance to) R is reflected by the magnitude of gain or penalty required to elicit the desired behavior. In some cases, the acts may be termed *assisted preferences:* once fear, advantage, and forecasts counsel a certain conduct, it may come to seem intrinsically worthwhile. And in other cases, behavior may be directly influenced by coercion, rewards, and predictions of R's eventual victory, without an adjustment of preferences. When T. E. Lawrence says:

> Rebellion . . . must have . . . a population . . . *sympathetic* to the point of not betraying rebel movements

[12] One indication of the degree of preference for R lies in the extent to which suppliers actually sell inputs to R **below** market prices, coercion aside.

[13] These influences are obviously connected closely with one another. Damage-limiting and profit-maximizing differ only in the **sign** of the outcome sought (minimizing loss versus maximizing gain); expectations, of course, affect **both.**

> to the enemy. Rebellions can be made by two percent
> active in a striking force, and 98 percent passively sym-
> pathetic . . .[14]

the relevant question is whether passive behavior (as well as
more active behavior) may not be largely explicable in terms of
damage-limiting, profit-maximizing, and inevitability (or probability) considerations rather than sympathy.

The degree to which behavior and sympathy can, in general,
diverge from one another is dramatically illustrated by the case
of Kitty Genovese, who was attacked and killed in New York
City in 1964 in the presence of 38 witnesses, none of whom
moved to assist her. And the case occurred not in the "third
world," but in the first; and not in the midst of a rural insurgency, but in the course of urban peace![15] How much more
likely is such behavior in the midst of an on-going rebellion?

To the extent that the population responds to damage-limiting motives, R's strength may derive directly from its harshness
toward uncongenial behavior. In Mao's words:

> In order to prevent the enemy relying on a hostile
> population from . . . making a surprise attack on us . . .
> *by methods of intimidation we warn the local popula-*
> *tion*, we arrest and detain people. [16]

To the extent that the population responds to profit-maximizing,
R should stress the rewards (opportunities, training, advance-
ment) of affiliation. And to the extent that the population's behavior is tied to expectations, R should emphasize its chances
and prospects rather than its merits. Guevara, for example,
forcefully suggests the dominance of predictions over preferences
by noting that:

> . . . the guerrilla [should] stress the unquestionable
> truth that those who hold out against the people *are*

[14] T. E. Lawrence, **Encyclopaedia Britannica**, 1950, Vol. X, 953.

[15] See A. M. Rosenthal, **Thirty-eight Witnesses** (New York: McGraw-Hill,
1964); **New York Times,** March 14 and 27, 1964.

[16] Mao Tse-tung, **Basic Tactics,** trans. by Stuart R. Schram, (New York:
Praeger, 1966), p. 119. Emphasis added.

going to lose. Anyone who does not feel this truth cannot be a guerrilla.[17]

And of course R may evoke the behavior it desires by methods that *combine* considerations of damage, gain, and prediction with appeals to higher values. Such adroit coordination is neatly suggested in the following statement by a member of the Viet Cong, who is explaining how he came to affiliate:

> They [the Viet Cong cadres] started by asking me to read the book *Youth Today.* In that book it was said that the youth's duty was to follow Uncle Ho's path in order to bring happiness to the people [higher values]. They told me that sooner or later I would be forced to do military service in the ARVN and we would be killed uselessly [forecasts, damage-limiting]. Therefore I had better join the Front forces. By doing so I would be able to resume my schooling and I will be able to become a physician or an engineer or to have a profession which would assure my future [profit-maximizing].[18]

Moreover, ascribing to preferences the behavior that is favorable to R tends to assume, or imply, that such motives themselves make the behavior in question worth more to R. On the contrary, fear (damage-limiting) and reward (profit-maximizing) may be as powerful spurs to desired behavior as are conscience and conviction. For example, when asked during an interview if he had had any special worries before he became active in the Front, one Viet Cong defector replied starkly:

> During the period 1960-1963 I was worried about being arrested and killed . . . by the Liberation Front people. . . . My father had been killed by them.[19]

Of course, the same pattern applies symmetrically to behavior desired by A. According to Bodard in his analysis of the French experience in Vietnam, civilians killed by the Viet Minh

---

[17] Guevara, **op. cit.,** pp. 11-12. Emphasis added.
[18] From a series of RAND interviews with former Viet Cong members.
[19] **Ibid.**

were often strong Vietminh sympathizers, "and nevertheless they frequently gave information to the police for money."[20]

To carry the point still further, when several Rs are competing for preeminence,[21] the rise of one of them to dominance does not necessarily imply that the populace prefers it—any more, and probably less, than the emergence of a monopoly from a prior phase of oligopoly necessarily implies that its particular brand is preferred by consumers. As noted earlier, consumer behavior will typically depend on the relative prices charged rather than on pure preferences, and emergent monopolists have been known to eliminate rivals by more nefarious means than price competition. In the case of rebellions, the emergent monopolist may assist preferences through damage-limiting (penalty) or profit-maximizing (price) influences, or by collaboration with A to eliminate rivals.[22] (The latter is a standard allegation when Rs compete, as unlikely to be always false as it is to be always true.)

Given the power of damage, gain, and expectations, an adroit R may manipulate its instrument panel in such a way that its popular support—in the sense of behavior benefiting it—rises while sympathy for its cause is falling. When, for example, Mrs. Aurora Quezon—the widow of a former president, and one of the most admired and popular figures in the Philippines—was killed by the Huks in the early 1950s, the attitude of the people toward the Huks became antagonistic. In the words of a Philippine army colonel, the attitude "changed over night."[23] Yet, according to Edward Lansdale:

> After her death, the Huks kept on recruiting and
> their forces did grow in size. . . . Their support from the

[20] Lucien Bodard, our translation, **La Guerre d'Indochine: II, l'Humiliation** (Paris: Editions Gallimard, 1965), 157.

[21] For example, in Batista's Cuba, the competition among Castro, Escalante, and other R groups; in Algeria, the struggle between the National Algerian Movement (MNA) and the National Liberation Front (FLN).

[22] See, for example, Hoang Van Chi's account of the feigned collaboration between Ho and the French police in the 1920s to eliminate Than Boi Chau's rival movement, the **Vietnam Quang-Phuc Hoi**, in **From Colonialism to Communism: A Case History of North Vietnam** (New York: Praeger, 1964), pp. 18-19.

[23] As quoted in A. H. Peterson, G. C. Reinhardt, and E. E. Conger, eds., **Symposium on the Role of Airpower in Counterinsurgency and Unconventional Warfare: The Philippine Huk Campaign,** The RAND Corporation, RM-3652-PR, June, 1963, Santa Monica, Calif., p. 21.

civilian population . . . grew after that, but . . . due to
. . . coercive methods. . . . [24]

Extrapolating, it would seem that an R may be victorious,
although sympathy for its cause is quite low. In the Irish Rebellion:

> In the Autumn of 1919 . . . IRA attacks on Crown
> forces were continually denounced in both the English
> and the Irish press as criminal outrages. The general
> mass of the Irish populace probably shared the view of
> the press and would have preferred the return of law
> and order to any dream of independence. [25]

The point applies symmetrically to A. Thus, A may block
and defeat a much-loved R, and even keep it defeated at low
maintenance costs, if only A's own resolve and resources seem
beyond doubt. Thus, the Soviet Union liquidated the Hungarian
rebellion without the population's preferences moving from R
toward A during the first years after 1956. More generally, A
may be able to reduce the military investment accompanying its
defeat of R, and do so with impunity, to the extent that the
former supporters of R predict that if R were to start again, they
would suffer large damage and to no avail. [26] For this forecast, A
must possess and convey its own sense of moral certitude, as
well as its capacity for effective action.

Furthermore, as noted earlier, the tension between preferences and sympathies on the one hand, and the perception of
dangers and opportunities (damage, reward, and prediction) on
the other, may lead to an adjustment of preferences. Sympathy
both for R and for A is not unrelated to their might and prospects. Clausewitz's observation that "public opinion is won

[24] **Ibid.**

[25] Edgar Holt, **Protest in Arms** (New York: Coward-McCann, 1960), p.
190. The preface to this book, incidentally, was written by the prominent Irish
revolutionary, Cathar O'Shannon.

[26] Contrast the conventional view expressed by Roger Hilsman before the
Senate Subcommittee on Refugees on September 30, 1965, that ". . . winning the
allegiance of the majority of the people . . . [is] in guerrilla warfare . . . the
only true and lasting victory." Hearings before the Subcommittee to Investigate
Problems Connected with Refugees and Escapees, United States Senate,
Refugee Problems in South Vietnam and Laos, Washington, U.S. Government
Printing Office, 1965, p. 318. Emphasis added.

through great victories"[27] is relevant to insurgent wars as well. Two separate but equally important influences may operate on opinion and behavior. First, the cause of the defeated or waning side may become unattractive from simple damage-limiting calculations. Moreover, for many, the defeated side is disgraced, perhaps less so in the West than in the area of Chinese culture, where the "Mandate of Heaven" is accorded or withheld according to fortune.[28] Although there are leads and lags accompanying this process, external pressure and tangible outcomes have a way of shaping convictions; the bandwagon (or "dominoes") effect has a moral as well as a cynical dimension.

Proposition 2: R derives its strength from poverty and inequality of income and wealth. (Conversely, if R is to be neutralized and A's strength enhanced or restored, poverty and inequality must be relieved.)

This is not the place for a full discussion of formal models of political change and its relation to economic change.[29] There are optimistic formulations suggesting that economic improvements increase the likelihood of congenial political change—for example, Coleman, Lerner, Hagen, and Robert McNamara.[30] There are pessimistic models suggesting the reverse relationship,

[27] See Karl von Clausewitz, **Principles of War** (Harrisburg, Pa.: Military Service Publishing Co., 1952), p. 46.

[28] The contrast between Orient and Occident on this point should not be exaggerated. Consider, for example, the Calvinist doctrine of "election" and the presumptive evidence of election that is provided by "success." See R. H. Tawney, **Religion and the Rise of Capitalism**, new ed., (New York: Harcourt Brace & World, 1947); Max Weber, **The Protestant Ethic and the Spirit of Capitalism** (New York: Scribner's Sons, 1948).

[29] Some of the relevant references include: Lawrence Stone, "Theories of Revolution," **World Politics**, Vol. XVIII, No. 2, January, 1966; S. M. Lipset, **Political Man; The Social Bases of Politics** (Garden City: Doubleday, 1959); J. L. Finkle and R. W. Gable, eds., **Political Development and Social Change** (New York: Wiley, 1966); Wolf, op. cit., Chapter 2.

[30] James S. Coleman, "The Political Systems of the Developing Areas," in G. A. Almond and J. S. Coleman, eds., **The Politics of the Developing Areas** (Princeton: Princeton University Press, 1960); Finkle and Gable, **op. cit.**, pp. 195-204; Everett E. Hagen, "A Framework for Analyzing Economic and Political Change," in Asher, Hagen, et al., **Development of the Emerging Countries** (Washington, D. C.: The Brookings Institution, 1962), pp. 1-38; McNamara, **op. cit.**

for example, Tocqueville, Hoffer, Feierabend, and Brinton. [31] And there are ambivalent models formulated in terms of various gaps between aspirations and performance, between wants and their satisfaction, and between prior and current rates of change. The ambivalent models usually lead to results that are indeterminate in the abstract, since they depend on the particular balance and interplay among a number of independent variables—for example, Davies, Smelser, and Wolf. [32] Without attempting such a critique, a few comments should be made that cast doubt on the validity of Proposition 2 in the insurgency context.

Historically the success or failure of insurgency has not borne a simple relationship to the degree of poverty. For example, living conditions in the early 1950s in Central Luzon, where the Hukbalahap were strong, appear to have been decidedly worse than economic conditions in various parts of Vietnam, particularly in the Delta region, where the Viet Cong were strong in the late 1950s. And yet the Huks could be defeated expeditiously and with moderate effort from within the Philippines; while in South Vietnam, despite a relatively lower level of deprivation and grievance on the part of the population, the Viet Cong would presumably have won in 1965 had it not been for massive American intervention. Indeed, economic conditions in South Vietnam were probably among the more favorable in Asia, just as Cuba was economically one of the more favorably situated countries in Latin America.

If one considers the matter in the more developed countries, a similar paradox holds. From an economic standpoint, Watts in 1965 was probably among the more favorably situated of the black communities in the U.S. When one looks at the Detroit riots of 1967, it turns out that incomes of rioters were significantly higher than those of non-rioters, after proper allowance has

[31] Alexis de Tocqueville, **The Old Regime and the French Revolution** (New York: Doubleday, 1955); Eric Hoffer, **The True Believer** (New York: Harper and Bros., 1951); Ivo K. and Rosalind L. Feierabend, "Aggressive Behaviors Within Polities, 1948-1962: A Cross-national Study," **Journal of Conflict Resolution,** Vol. X, No. 3, September, 1966; Crane Brinton, **The Anatomy of Revolution,** rev. ed., (New York: Vintage Books, 1965).

[32] James C. Davies, "Toward a Theory of Revolution," **American Sociological Review,** Vol. 27, No. 1, February, 1962; See Finkle and Gable, **op. cit.,** pp. 28-44; Charles Wolf, Jr., **Foreign Aid: Theory and Practice in Southern Asia** (Princeton: Princeton University Press, 1960), Chapter 8.

been made for differences in the age distributions of the two groups.[33] Similarly, campus rebellions have often been most severe in those academic centers (for example, Berkeley, Columbia, Wisconsin, Cornell, Harvard and Swarthmore) where living and learning conditions were among the best.

When one looks at rates of change, rather than levels, in the relevant economic variables, the proposition comes no closer to reality. In the Philippines, rates of change were negative or low; in Vietnam, positive and relatively high. A striking example of the Tocquevillean hypothesis (that improvements may abet revolution) is conveyed in a description of conditions preceding the Mau Mau insurgency in Kenya:

> In 1945, the inhabitants of the Kikuyu Reserve were . . . more prosperous than ever before. . . . The Kikuyu had done well out of the war. . . . The population . . . was for the first time cooperating well with the . . . agricultural policies being promoted by the government to increase the productivity of what land they had. . . . Terracing, improved irrigation, cattle dipping and other new ideas formerly opposed were now being accepted. In his annual report for 1945 the Provincial Commissioner, Central Province [in which the Kikuyu reserve lies], could allow himself the unaccustomed luxury of a guarded optimism: ". . . during the last few years the native reserves have experienced an unparalleled wave of . . . prosperity."[34]

Of course, anecdotes neither destroy nor validate relationships, since the latter may apply in a large number of excluded cases. But there is a more fundamental reason for viewing the proposition with considerable doubt, including its operational implication that economic improvement programs contribute to recouping or enhancing A's strength. The usual presumption is that such benefits will increase the sympathy or preferences of the population in favor of A, and thereby conduce to behavior congenial to the government. Although the effects of such improvements are likely to be sensitive to the criteria used in deter-

---

[33] We are indebted for this point to work done by Albert Wohlstetter and Sinclair Coleman, which will be published soon.

[34] Fred Majdalany, **State of Emergency** (London: Longmans Green, 1962), p. 56.

mining the kind and location of projects,[35] the typical result is likely to be drastically different from the intended one.

The reason is not hard to find. Economic improvement programs, while they *may* affect the preferences of the populace, as between A and R, *will* influence the resources available to the population for satisfying its preferences. In the language of economics, there is an income effect that may offset and outweigh the preference effect. Even if an individual's preference for A is increased, the fact that he commands additional income as a result of economic improvement enables him to use some of this increased income to "buy" his security or protection from R, thereby making him feel that he is improving his chances of survival. Even if the population were hostile toward R—short of an unlikely intensity of hostility that might lead to denouncing and combatting R—both the population and R can benefit from economic improvement efforts undertaken by A. Some U.S. economic aid projects in Vietnam have almost certainly helped the Viet Cong.

From the standpoint of an adroit R, the options opened to it by economic improvement programs of A are impressive. At one extreme, from the point of view of the populace, R may transform the benefits provided by A from boons into dangers by threatening the recipients. For example, commenting on the consequences of land reform by the South Vietnamese government, one report noted:

> Often the peasants ask Saigon *not* to give them legal title to their land—in case the Viet Cong should come back and find out. [36]

R may also undo the benefits conferred by A by destroying them, [37] by appropriating them, [38] or by taxing the resulting in-

[35] See this chapter, pp. 20-21, and Appendix.

[36] **The Economist,** July 9, 1966, p. 131.

[37] As noted by Bernard Fall, "A promising malaria eradication program was stopped late in 1961 because of the casualties among its personnel (22 killed and 60 kidnapped in less than one year) and the losses of equipment." In **The Two Vietnams** (New York: Praeger, 1966), p. 361.

[38] According to a **New York Times** report of August 15, 1964: "In many parts of the country, American field workers complete a technical aid project, a bridge, road or well, only to have the guerrillas occupy the village the moment the Americans and Vietnamese co-workers pull out." Quoted in Robert Taber, **The War of the Flea: A Study of Guerrilla Warfare Theory and Practice** (New York: Lyle Stuart, 1965), p. 88.

crease in income. And if R is content to share the increase in income with the populace, the negative worth of this to A may exceed the positive worth, if any, from increased popular preference for A.

The bizarre way in which A's improvement projects can work to the benefit of R is suggested in a report on Vietnam by Denis Warner:

> The Viet Cong freely circulated in the villages where the government's pacification plan had high priority. . . . "Quang Nam's pacification project has become a sort of Viet Cong-dependent aid area financed by the Americans," said one U.S. official. "We've even found a letter written from a mother inside the area to her son with the Viet Cong telling him not to worry about her, that she is being looked after just fine and he can cheerfully get on with the fighting."[39]

If a side undertaking economic improvement is to avert an unfavorable outcome from the interplay between a *certain* income effect and an *uncertain* preference effect, the criteria according to which economic improvement projects are selected and administered must be modified. Where the familiar criteria of productivity and equity are applied, the certainty of increased income may well offset the uncertainty of strengthened preferences, to the disadvantage of the side in question. The problem is how to make the increased income depend on behavior desired by the side undertaking the improvement projects. Thus, the relative price of *un*desirable behavior should be made to rise, with a resulting tendency to *substitute* desirable for undesirable behavior.[40] For this substitution effect to operate, a side must be able to distinguish among different kinds of behavior, and act accordingly—capabilities that add to the side's requirements for information and intelligence.[41] Without such capabilities,

[39] Denis Warner, "Showdown in Danang," **The Reporter,** June 2, 1966, p. 15.
[40] See Chapter 3, pp. 37-38.
[41] See Chapter 7.

economic improvement measures are as apt to hinder as to help. [42]

Turning from economic improvement to social equality does not provide much stronger ground for optimism. In some and perhaps many historical instances, reform and redistribution were already underway when the rebellion got up steam. Tocqueville's observations are well-known about the effects of more equitable taxation and "right-to-work" edicts in fostering rather than easing revolutionary ferment during the decline and fall of the *ancien régime*. (And this effect was probably not entirely due to the fact that promises exceeded performance.) [43] Data on the *level* of equality, rather than changes (reforms), point in the same direction. A recent study suggests that insurgent control in Vietnam in 1964-1965 was more likely to be strong in areas where land holdings in prior years had been of more equal size, and tenant cultivation—rather than owner cultivation—had been less prevalent. [44] Moreover, allowance for *changes* toward greater equality tended to strengthen these results. [45]

> *Proposition 3:* In the growth of R and in its prospects for success, factors and influences that are fundamentally internal *(endogeny)* predominate over factors and influences that are external *(exogeny)*. (Conversely, for A to prevent or defeat R, its efforts and counterpressures must place primary emphasis on endogenous rather than exogenous targets.)

There is a logical as well as a functional connection between Proposition 3 (endogeny versus exogeny) on the one hand and Propositions 1 (popular support) and 2 (economic deprivation) on the other. The connection is based on the implicit (and questionable) premise that the strength of an influence diminishes

---

[42] The Appendix to this chapter sharpens the distinctions among the income, preference, and substitution effects, based on the theory of consumer behavior.

[43] Taxes, for example, apparently **were** collected more equitably in prerevolutionary France than they had been earlier. Cf. Tocqueville, **op. cit.**, pp. 180-181 ff.

[44] Edward J. Mitchell, "Inequality and Insurgency: A Statistical Study of South Vietnam," **World Politics**, Vol. XX, No. 3, April, 1968, 421-438.

[45] **Ibid.**

with its distance from the object it is influencing.[46] An external source of influence (for example, North Vietnam, China, or the Soviet Union in relation to South Vietnam) is constrained—and in some versions of the premise precluded—from effectively influencing the population, or the economic conditions on which the presumed support for R depends, by the remoteness of that external source compared with the proximity of endogenous sources. Consequently, if popular support and economic deprivation are the crucial ingredients in R's rise, then it follows that endogeny should predominate over exogeny. Moreover, to the extent that exogeny operates at all, Proposition 3 implies a phylogenetic law: *endogeny begets exogeny*, rather than vice versa. The willingness of external sources to contribute to a rebellion depends on that rebellion's internal strength.

In an exchange of views on Vietnam between the foreign editor of the London *Economist* and his counterpart on the Polish weekly journal *Polityka*, the Polish editor plainly formulated the primacy of endogeny over (an almost negligible) exogeny:

> Your [the *Economist*] argument that "the decision to start the Viet Cong rebellion was taken in Hanoi" is founded on the strange belief that every revolution and every struggle for national liberation is the result of instigation from outside. This view is quite false, and it is contradicted by the historic experience of the past 50 years. . . . It will make no difference whether or not the Democratic Republic of Vietnam assists the insurgents. Even if—to take a theoretical case—Ho Chi Minh were to appeal to the National Liberation Front to surrender, I do not believe that the insurgents would comply.[47]

Frequent use of the term "civil war" to describe R evokes a

---

[46] There is an interesting parallel between the endogeny-versus-exogeny position in the insurgency context and the decline-in-power-with-increasing-distance hypothesis in connection with other wars. See Kenneth E. Boulding, **Conflict and Defense** (New York: Harper and Row, 1962), pp. 78-79 ff. As Wohlstetter has shown, the hypothesis does not apply in conventional wars or nuclear contingencies. Its applicability in the insurgency context is equally weak. See Albert Wohlstetter, "Illusions of Distance," **Foreign Affairs**, Vol. 46, No. 2, January, 1968. For an earlier demonstration of this point, see Eugene Staley, "Myth of the Continents," **Foreign Affairs**, Vol. XIX, April, 1941, 481-494.

[47] **The Economist,** December 11, 1965, p. 1180.

similar picture of the primacy of endogeny. However, sometimes the term refers to an ethnic or historical, rather than a political, propinquity, which makes "endogeny" more inclusive. Help or direction from North Vietnam may then be considered quite consistent with an "endogenous" view of the Viet Cong. Thus, in the words of a participant in a debate on Vietnam in the United States Senate:

> . . . you can look at the war in Vietnam as a covert invasion of the south by the north, or . . . as basically an indigenous war . . . but either way it is a war between Vietnamese to determine what the ultimate kind of government is going to be for Vietnam. When I went to school that was a civil war.[48]

In Proposition 3 as in Proposition 1, the emergence and progress of R appears analogous to a popular election in which the showing of each party depends on, and reflects, popular preferences. Indeed, R's emergence is itself often viewed as a reflection of A's loss of a preliminary heat in a subliminal popularity contest determined by endogeny. The outcome of these influences is analogous to the progress of an electoral campaign: the population judges the contest and expresses the preferences that determine its outcome; external influences are largely irrelevant.

Among the endogenous factors that are viewed as crucial are the characteristics of internal political leadership, an ingredient that allegedly cannot be provided or manipulated externally. The hearts-and-minds view underlying Proposition 3 often asserts that a necessary condition for an A to defeat a contemporary R is a charismatic figure indelibly marked with a populist image. Leadership must be provided by the kind of "man of the people" that Ramon Magsaysay was (or perhaps has been transformed into, through a process of building a legend around a core of truth). In this role, a westernized hedonist like Nguyen Cao Ky would be clearly inappropriate (as would an unreconstructed Catholic mandarin like Ngo Dinh Diem).

What can be said about the validity of endogeny-over-

---

[48] Remarks of Senator Frank Church, Hearings before the Committee on Foreign Relations, United States Senate, **Supplemental Foreign Assistance, Fiscal Year 1966—Vietnam,** Washington, U.S. Government Printing Office, 1966, p. 47.

exogeny? In one sense, it is inescapably correct, although truistic. There must be some endogenous issues, people, and opportunities, or else R becomes either a raiding party (for example, Indonesia's abortive R in Malaysia in 1963-1965) or an invasion (the Korean war). But what is the *balance* between endogeny and exogeny in a typical R, and how does that balance change over time?

The possibilities and examples are numerous. In some cases, such as Cuba, exogeny may be negligible in size and relatively unimportant; the weakness of the authority structure and the strength of endogeny may be determinative without exogeny. In others, such as South Vietnam and conceivably Thailand, the extent and importance of exogenous direction, leadership, training, and support may be great (for A as well as for R). Other cases lie in between—Malaya, perhaps closer to Vietnam, and the Philippines, perhaps closer to Cuba. Tradeoffs between exogeny and endogeny are possible; different combinations can generate a successful or an unsuccessful R, as the following statement by an observer in Vietnam suggests:

> "When a people's war gets important and sustained outside help, even an unusually vigorous government will likely lose unless it can choke off this foreign support. Conversely, a rather weak government can usually suppress a people's war if the rebels are cut off from all outside help.[49]

Nevertheless, while substantial exogeny is neither necessary nor sufficient for successful R, an ambiguous history seems to suggest that R has never been suppressed *unless* external help has previously been terminated. R *may* win without external support; A is unlikely to win if R continues to receive it.[50]

In summary, then, the set of views we have been describing: (a) pays almost sole attention to popular support based on ardor and preferences, (b) views economic deprivation and its amelioration as dominant influences on the strength of R and A, and (c) stresses endogeny and minimizes exogeny. Perceiving the conflict between R and A as analogous to an election, such views regard

---

[49] John Randolph, **Los Angeles Times,** March 19, 1967.

[50] See Chapter 5, pp. 76-77, for a discussion of barriers and border control to inhibit exogeny in counterinsurgency operations.

indigenous, populist, charismatic leadership as a necessary condition for A's victory.

These views have been starkly drawn; they are rarely discussed in terms quite so sharp. They lead to the acceptance and endorsement of such slogans as "counterinsurgency is a political rather than a military struggle," and "a battle for the hearts and minds of the people." They stand in contrast to an alternative approach, to which we turn in the next chapter.

Appendix to Chapter 2

Income, Preference, and Substitution Effects of Economic Improvement

Consider a villager (consumer) subject to the opposing pressures (appeals) of A and R. The two axes shown below represent payments (in taxes and effort) by the villager to A and R, respectively, for protection, services, tribute, and the like.

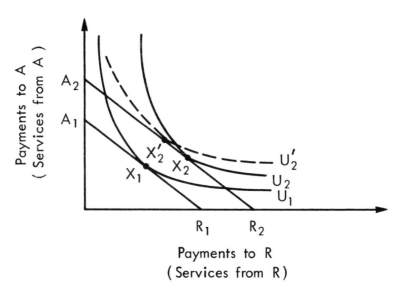

Payments to R
(Services from R)

$A_1 R_1$ is the initial locus of options ("budget line") open to the villager. Depending on his preference function (shown by the convex isoquants U_1, U_2), he will choose to be somewhere along $A_1 R_1$, such as X_1.

Next, economic improvement raises the budget line to $A_2 R_2$. If preferences are unchanged, the villager's new equilibrium point is X_2 (a pure income effect). Both R and A will benefit, and R may benefit more than A as the figure illustrates.

If his preferences are changed, the slope of the preference map may change in A's favor, with isoquants becoming flatter as shown by U_2'. The villager would now rather pay to A than to

R, or receive services from A than R. If utility (satisfaction) is held constant, a unit paid to A (or services received from A) by the villager is worth more than before in terms of units paid to R. His new equilibrium is at X'_2, and this outcome may be less (more) favorable to A if the preference effect is weaker (stronger) than the income effect (or if the negative worth to A of the increased payments to R exceeds (falls short of) the value to A of its increased receipts).

If, however, the *terms* are altered on which the villager's increase in income is made available to him—reflected by the fact, perhaps, that improvement projects are allocated to those who cooperate but not to those who do not—then the budget line pivots clockwise from A_2R_2 to $A_2R'_2$.

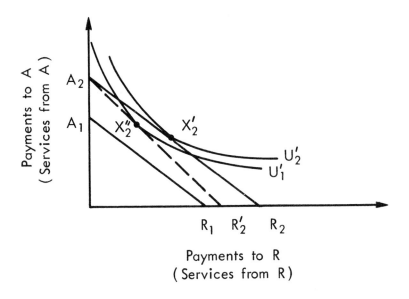

The villager's equilibrium now moves to X''_2, relatively more favorable to A because of a substitution of A-buying for R-buying (the substitution effect).

Chapter 3

AN ALTERNATIVE APPROACH: INSURGENCY AS A SYSTEM

The hearts-and-minds view of rebellion is that of the outsider looking in. In its stress on popular sympathies and economic conditions, it concentrates on the environment that evokes R and causes it to emerge and grow, more or less spontaneously. Its emphasis is on the demand side of the problem. To transpose an analogy from economics, the hearts-and-minds view is a *demand-pull* version of the process, whereas the view we shall be presenting is more in the nature of a *cost-push* version. Our view will, to a greater extent, emphasize factors within the insurgent organization which influence its capabilities and growth. It will thus place somewhat greater emphasis on the supply (production) side of R's growth, and the bearing of supply considerations on the prevention or defeat of R.

Of course, behavior depends on interactions *between* supply and demand. Both need to be considered in understanding population behavior in the insurgency context, no less than consumer behavior in the marketplace. We offer two reasons for placing somewhat more emphasis on supply. One is that, while both demand and supply are important, we feel that in most discussions supply factors have either been neglected or misconstrued. In the theory of consumer behavior, to revert to the economic analogy, it is customary to distinguish between the effect of consumer preferences (demand conditions) and the possibilities for buying different commodities as reflected by their relative costs (supply conditions). The interaction between them determines market behavior. By contrast, the hearts-and-minds analysis focuses principal attention on the preferences, attitudes, and sympathies of the populace (demand), to the neglect of the opportunities and costs required to indulge these preferences.[1] Similarly, in discussions of campus rebellions, principal attention is often focussed on student demands and grievances, rather than on the actions (or inaction) of administrators and faculty that lower the costs and facilitate the organization and radicalization of student rebellion.

The second reason is that supply conditions are probably more elastic (responsive)—at least in the short run—to programs and policies than are demand conditions, especially from A's point of view. Dealing with the demand conditions in the less developed countries involves the massive problems of modernization, and in the more developed countries the problems of reform that are only less massive in a relative sense. It is important and necessary to grapple with these problems (among other reasons, so that A can sustain its own sense of rectitude and purpose). Nevertheless, the problems are apt to be unyielding in the short run. The progress that can realistically be aimed for will probably leave the demand for R fairly strong, especially if —as seems likely—progress lags behind promises.[2] This prospect presents an asymmetrical advantage to R. It may be much easier for R to activate and enhance a potential demand for itself than for A to reduce this demand. Thus, demand may be harder to shift downward than upward. Hence, while *both* A and R must attend sharply to the supply or production side of the problem, A may have less leverage on the demand side than R. Hence, it may be efficient for R to allocate relatively more resources to influencing the demand side, and for A to allocate more to the supply side.

Fundamental to our analysis is the assumption that the population, as individuals or groups, behaves "rationally": that it calculates costs and benefits to the extent that they can be related to different courses of action, and makes choices accordingly. Apparent irrationalities can be explained by mistakes; uncertainties; misinformation; a shortage of information on the part of

---

[1] For clarification of the demand/supply distinction, and the important interactions between them, see pp. 37-39.

[2] See this chapter, pp. 30-32.

the population; or a misunderstanding on the observer's part of how the population weighs different things in its calculations. Consequently, influencing popular behavior requires neither sympathy nor mysticism, but rather a better understanding of what costs and benefits the individual or the group is concerned with, and how they are calculated. The rationality assumption is admittedly an oversimplification. Its justification hopefully lies in helping to analyze a subject that has often been treated in an obscure, if not obscurantist, way.

The following discussion will describe our alternative approach in terms of three elements: (1) the environment of the less developed countries, (2) the insurgency—R—as a system, and (3) the individual or group in relation to R. Finally, contrasts are drawn between the alternative approach and the hearts-and-minds view discussed in Chapter 2.

The Environment

Traditional societies that have begun to change provide, by the process of change itself, opportunities for insurgent movements.[3] (And societies in which the structure of traditional authority remains intact potentially provide the same opportunities, to the extent that change lies ahead of them.) Endemic, if latent, cleavages and antagonisms tend to be inflamed once the transition to modernization has begun—antagonisms between landlords and tenants; between urban and rural areas; among ethnic, racial, religious, and linguistic groups. Inequities in the distribution of wealth, income, education, and opportunity are chronic and widespread, and the pain that accompanies them is often felt more acutely as modernization begins to open up the possibility of remedies and evoke promises and aspirations that move ahead of the remedies. Resentment against the privilege

[3] That change exposes and intensifies vulnerabilities to insurgency is, of course, not confined to traditional societies. Thus, in the United States during the past decade, the most rapid improvements in civil rights since the Civil War have been followed or accompanied by the most violent resistance to the residual, if declining, discrimination. Eric Hoffer has eloquently and exhaustively examined the phenomenon in his various works. See, for example, **The True Believer** (New York: Harper & Bros., 1951); **The Passionate State of Mind** (New York: Harper & Row, 1955); and **The Ordeal of Change** (New York: Harper & Row, 1963). For another penetrating exposition, see Robert Waelder, **Progress and Revolution** (New York: International Universities Press, 1967).

and status enjoyed by foreigners as a colonial legacy, or by domestic elites as a legacy of traditional society, is often acute or easily aroused. Such patterns of bitterness and resentment are as much a part of the realities of transitional societies as are low income levels, and they are very likely to intensify as income levels rise—other things being equal—at least up to some threshold. As one experienced observer summarizes the point:

> Every insurgency . . . requires a cause. [But] there is always some issue which has an appeal to each section of the community, and, even if dormant, an inspired incident may easily revive it in an acute form. . . . All governments are vulnerable to criticism, and every grievance, shortcoming or abuse will be exploited. [4]

Although the preceding point applies with particular force in the less developed countries, it is relevant in the more developed countries, too. Thus Sidney Hook comments on disruption in university campuses in the United States:

> On every campus there are always some grievances. Instead of seeking peacefully to resolve them through existing channels of consultation and deliberation, the SDS [Students for a Democratic Society] seeks to inflame them. Where grievances don't exist, they can be created. In one piece of advice to chapter members, they were urged to sign up for certain courses in large numbers, and then denounce the University for its large classes! [5]

Another characteristic of the less developed countries that enhances their vulnerability to insurgency is the mutual isolation of their component parts. Less developed countries are "plural" economic and social entities in the sense that they contain units that are physically, as well as functionally and technologically, remote from one another. Villages, districts, towns, provinces, and cities are in imperfect and intermittent contact. They are often in isolation from one another and particularly from the capital city and the institutions of the central government concentrated there. Thus, flows of commodities, information, and

---

[4] Thompson, **op. cit.,** pp. 21-22.
[5] In "The Prospects of Academe," **Encounter,** August, 1968, p. 62.

people from place to place are extremely limited. Because the links and contacts among these enclaves, and between them and the center, are meager, the ability of an A to maintain surveillance and establish control over an inchoate insurgency is accordingly limited. The difficulty (that is, the high cost) of obtaining reliable and timely information—which A needs more than does R—is highly correlated with many other structural characteristics of the less developed countries—for example, per capita income, urbanization, literacy, longevity, industrialization, and political participation. But from the standpoint of the circumstances that facilitate R's emergence, the high cost of information and communication may be considerably more significant than other typical attributes of the environment in less developed countries.[6]

Given these characteristics, it is a truism to say that transitional societies are vulnerable to insurgency. Changing the characteristics is complex and time-consuming. Moreover, the *process* of modernization itself by no means reduces the vulnerabilities in question, although that is more likely to be the *outcome* of modernization in the longer run. For these reasons, it is wise to separate the analysis of R from that of development and modernization in general. To analyze and understand R in the less developed countries, we need to factor it out of the wider set of modernization problems to which it is related. Focusing on R leads to viewing it as a system.

Rebellion as a System

What does it mean to view an insurgent movement as a system? The alternative approach to be explored here starts with the observation that insurgent movements, as operating systems, require that certain inputs—obtained from either internal or external sources—be converted into certain outputs, or activities. These activities characterize the stage to which R has progressed.

In general, insurgency requires inputs of recruits, information, shelter, and food—almost always obtained from the internal

---

[6] See Chapter 7, pp. 132-137. Although the characteristics we have been describing typify the less developed, transitional countries, they are not entirely excluded from the more developed countries. Watts and Appalachia are LDC pockets within an MDC garment. While opportunities for insurgency are more limited in the MDCs, they are not absent.

environment (endogeny)—and cadres, publicity, material, and initial financing—often provided from external sources (exogeny).[7] The "mix" between endogeny and exogeny is variable: it differs between different Rs, and in the same R at different times. To obtain inputs from the local environment, R relies on various persuasive as well as coercive (damage-threatening or damage-inflicting) techniques.[8] In practice, both persuasion and coercion are important as well as intimately linked. Severe coercion is often combined with a considerable and effective persuasive effort by Rs.[9]

Persuasion may take many forms: ideological preparation, education, discrediting of established authority and practices,[10] and payment (rewards). Coercion may also take many forms: the threat and carrying out of kidnapping, assassination, torture, forcible tax collection, and destruction or confiscation of property, including crop and land seizure. Often coercion and persuasion are mixed, as, for example, in compulsory assemblies for group criticism and self-criticism. Again, the actual and the efficient combination between persuasion and coercion are important to study, in order to understand both the organization and operation of R and the problem of countering R. Certain hypotheses can be examined concerning mixes of coercion and persuasion that may be effective in influencing different types of individuals or groups. For example, coercion may be more effective in obtaining compliance from the "haves," who initially are relatively favored and hence have something appreciable to lose; while persuasion and inducements may be more effective in obtaining compliance from the disadvantaged, who have little to lose and may therefore tend to cherish, and perhaps magnify, any gains by comparison. Of course, a mixture of the two may be more effective than either alone, but the proportions in the mix will vary with the circumstances of the intended target.

The inputs acquired by combining persuasion and coercion

[7] See Chapter 2, pp. 21-24.

[8] Discussed more fully in Chapters 4 and 6.

[9] R's effective use of persuasion is closely related to the asymmetrical quality of the demand for rebellion, alluded to earlier: such demand may be easier to shift upward than downward. See p. 29.

[10] For any set of implementers of authority (officials, policemen, military personnel) there will always be a lower-performing segment whose discredit is easier and more appropriate for R to target.

are converted into outputs by the insurgent organization. As with many organizations, R tends to organize personnel, financial, logistics, intelligence, communications, and operations branches to manage the conversion of inputs into activities; and it uses a wide range of incentives (recognition, reward, promotion) and penalties (criticism, isolation, demotion, and physical punishment) to spur the operations of these branches.

The outputs or activities of R include acts of sabotage, violence against individuals, public demonstrations, small-scale attacks, and eventually larger attacks and mobile warfare, on the military side. But R's outputs also include the exercise of administrative and governmental jurisdiction (village aid projects, education and training, formation of youth and other organizations concerned with group action programs). The aim of R's activities is to demonstrate that A is immoral, incompetent, and impotent —that A is, in other words, undeserving and a loser.

The view of insurgency described here can be summarized in Figure 1.

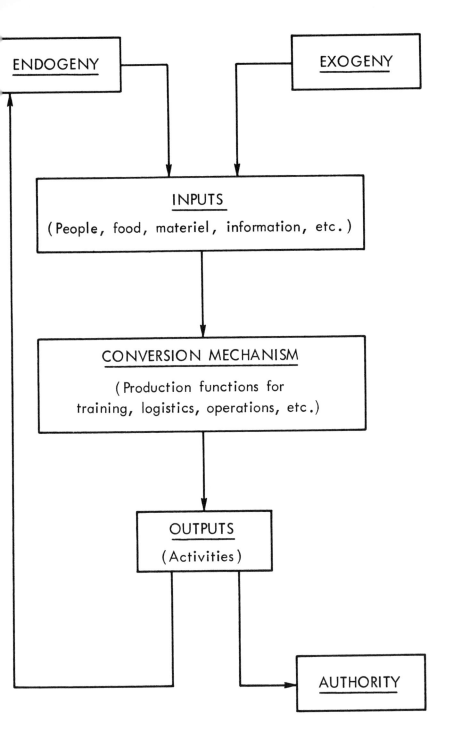

Fig. 1—Insurgency as a system

The systems view of insurgency enables one to distinguish four methods of counterinsurgency which will be summarized here and elaborated later.[11] The first is to raise the cost to R of obtaining inputs, or reduce the inputs obtained for given costs: the aim is input-denial. The second is to impede the process by which R converts these inputs into activities—that is, to reduce the efficiency of R's production process. The third is to destroy R's outputs. And the fourth is to blunt the effects of R's outputs on the population and on A—that is, to increase A's and the population's capacity to absorb R's activities.

The first two methods may be termed "counterproduction," which hinders R's production of activities by either denying inputs or changing the production coefficients so that smaller outputs are generated from given inputs.

Examples of the first method, input-denial, include interdiction by air, ground, or naval action; construction of barriers that impede the movement of people or supplies from a source to a destination; and preemptive buying programs that try to engage the available suppliers of particular inputs (such as rice) so that these goods are less readily available to R.

Efforts by A to reduce R's productive efficiency (the second method) include creating distrust and frictions within R's organization by planting rumors; attracting defectors (particularly those from the higher ranks in R's civil and military organization); disseminating credible misinformation about the behavior of R's leadership; and generally raising the noise level in R's information system.

The third method is the traditional counterforce role of military action. Besides the application of firepower from ground and air, it depends especially on accurate intelligence, so that targeting error in the use of such firepower is reduced. Otherwise, such error is likely to be high because targets are closely collocated with the people. (The importance of intelligence to reduce targeting error in counterforce operations can hardly be overemphasized, and we shall return to it later.)[12]

The fourth method, increasing A's and the population's capacity to absorb the outputs of R, is analogous to passive and

[11] See Chapter 5, pp. 76-83.

active defense in strategic analysis. [13] Its passive-defensive aspects include such measures as building village fortifications ("hardening"), and relocating villagers so that they are less accessible to R (evacuation). Its active-defensive aspects involve creating or strengthening local paramilitary and police units with increased capacity to provide local defense against small unit actions by R. In the realm of political action, such capacity requires (1) A's adherence to law and order in contrast to R, and (2) its demonstrated ability to complete announced programs, thereby certifying that it *should* govern because it *is* governing.

How different is this approach from the one associated with the hearts-and-minds doctrine? Admittedly the differences are of degree rather than kind. But the differences of degree involve an important degree of difference. One contrast is to lay greater stress, in dealing with problems of counterinsurgency, on the supply side of insurgency (for example, on how the R system obtains its inputs, from what sources, in what quantities, in return for what persuasive, coercive, or inducement measures, how it manages these inputs and converts them into the system's outputs) rather than on the demand side (how receptive the feelings of the population are to an insurgency).

The supply side of the problem relates to the difficulty or cost of producing R's activities; the higher these costs, the lower the scale or the probability of R. The demand side of the problem relates to what people are willing to pay (or contribute) for R's activities. The more they want an insurgency, the higher the price they will pay for these activities; hence, the greater the scale or the probability of R.[14] But for given preferences or desires, the price people will be willing to pay depends also on the resources they have available and the terms under which contributions toward an insurgency might be made (that is, the risks of damage or hopes of gain that enter into their calculations).

When counterrebellion operates on the supply side, the aim is to make the cost of R exceed the price that its internal or

[13] Cf. Robert Levine, **The Arms Debate** (Cambridge: Harvard University Press, 1963), pp. 229-233, 240-243, 309; Herman Kahn, **On Thermonuclear War** (Princeton: Princeton University Press, 1960), pp. 126-144, 303-304, 518-521.

[14] See the earlier discussion of income and substitution effects in Chapter 2, pp. 19-20. See also the Appendix to chapter 3, pp. 46-47.

external supporters are willing to pay to support it, especially at
high levels of activity. When counterrebellion operates on the demand side, it tries to reduce what people are willing to pay for R
activities. Stressing the supply side means trying to raise the costs
of producing R's activities, hence raising the costs of reaching a
given scale or probability of rebellion. The analysis presented
here places relatively greater emphasis on the supply than on the
demand side, while the reverse applies to the hearts-and-minds
orientation.[15]

While the demand-supply distinction helps clarify the contrasts between orientations, there are important interactions between demand and supply that should not be overlooked. The
difficulty or cost of operating R and increasing its strength depends, as discussed earlier, on its access to various inputs provided by the population. The population's demand function
influences that access and the terms on which it is obtained. For
example, if demand rises, the costs of information and recruits
may get lower (the supply function may fall). Conversely, if costs
are increased, the demand function may fall. In effect, demand
exercises an influence on supply, and vice versa.

This problem is also familiar in economics, although there
too the usual demand-supply dichotomy often ignores interactions between the two.[16] But several particular points should be

---

[15] In formal terms, the distinction between demand and supply relates to
two functions:

$$D = D(p, x_i)$$
$$S = S(c, y_j)$$

D is the quantity of R activities that will be bought; p is the price per unit. S is
the R activities produced; c is the cost per unit; x_i and y_j are other influences on
demand and supply, respectively. (Both D and S can be disaggregated into endogenous and exogenous components.) The intersection between D and S determines the scale of R, or, from another standpoint, the probability of R.

The demand curve is likely to be "kinked" at both high and low price
levels (because of a shortage of wholly committed, ardent supporters at high
levels, and the "bandwagon" effect at low levels), and hard to shift (inelastic
with respect to policies and programs). The supply curve may have a negative
second derivative and later an inflection point because of economies of scale and
efficiencies from "learning-by-doing."

[16] The interactions can operate both through the effects of **shifts** in demand
on the supply function, and through **movements** along a given demand function.
For example, shifting demand functions may stimulate (or discourage) research
and development, and the emergence of technological change that influences supply. And movements along a given demand function can cause suppliers to
accelerate (or decelerate) cost-reducing innovations. Where sellers and buyers
are numerous and atomistic, the interactions are weakened.

noted about the demand-supply interaction in the insurgency context. The demand that is operative in the sense of influencing R's supply function may, as discussed earlier, be confined to a small segment of the population. And the adroitness of R itself, as well as A's maladroitness, can activate and stimulate popular demand.[17] What is at work is a network of positive feedbacks: the population's effective demands influence the costs and effectiveness of R's activities, and R's activities influence (by the manipulation of both persuasion and coercion)[18] the population's demands. Conversely, clumsy reactions and overreactions by A to provocation from R can intensify popular demand. The discussion of provocation by R and "hot" violence by A, in Chapter 6, provides examples of this type of interaction.

Another contrast lies in the different view of endogeny and exogeny which emerges. Hearts-and-minds stresses nearly pure endogeny,[19] whereas the systems approach views the problem in terms of tradeoffs between the two. The inputs that the R system requires can be provided from internal or external sources, in combinations that may vary at different times in the same insurgency, and in different insurgencies. Internal sources can be primary, in the sense that they provide a larger (or more valuable) share of the total input than does exogeny, or they can be secondary.[20] Moreover, the value of external (or internal) inputs cannot be inferred from their bulk, or their market prices. For example, external provision of leadership, money, intelligence, training, sanctuary, propaganda, and diplomatic pressure may have an importance in the emergence and growth of R which is not adequately measured by the flow of tons of sup-

---

[17] See the statements by Thompson and Hook, footnote 4, this chapter.

[18] See Chapter 6.

[19] Fulbright, **op. cit.**; Hilsman, **op. cit.**; Halberstam, **op. cit.**

[20] It is another question whether the level of, and changes in, the exogeny/endogeny ratio may not be highly important for U.S. policy. It may be the case that those Rs in which U.S. political interests are most involved are likely to be cases in which the ratio is large, or is rising. However, one must be careful about imputing too much significance to this ratio, inasmuch as it can change over time. Furthermore, there are likely to be considerable lags between the achievement of a particular level and the flow and processing of information relating to it. Hence, what was at one time a high exogeny/endogeny ratio may have, by the time the relevant information reaches a decision point in A's bureaucracy, already become substantially lower.

plies, or numbers of people, across a contiguous border.[21] Thus, while the problem of internal versus external sources is more likely to arise in terms of the mix between two sources of inputs, successful counterrebellion has always required either the absence of significant external support (for example, the Philippines and Malaya) or the shutting off of such support (Greece and Algeria). This is consistent with the fact that there have been cases of successful insurgency *without* such external support (Cuba), where the authority was weak and ineffectual. Curtailing exogeny is necessary but not sufficient for successful counterrebellion.

Even if one assumes the primacy of endogeny, the systems approach leads to different implications from those associated with the hearts-and-minds approach. The central questions include not only popular attitudes, but also R's operations: how R obtains its supplies; what forms of coercion and persuasion are used to influence the population; how R makes payments and raises revenues. Whether one wants to control R, or to strengthen or replicate it, the *inside* of R is what needs to be studied. While one wants to know something about the market within which R operates, under the systems approach one is especially concerned with how R operates within that environment, and with the difference between a successful and a less successful R in such operations (that is, an "interfirm" contrast).

Consider the analogy between two firms, F_1 and F_2, producing the same product in two noncompeting markets, M_1 and M_2. If, at the end of a period, F_1 shows high output, low cost, and high profit, should we say that the explanation for its success relative to F_2 is due to differences in conditions *within the market* M_1, compared with M_2?

Sometimes this may be so, and if it is we would look principally to differences in demand conditions in the two markets —hence, in consumer preferences and income—for the explanation. But our analysis would be incomplete if we did not look as well to possible differences *within the firms*, F_1 and F_2, to account for their different degrees of success. For example, we might find that management in F_1 is superior to that in F_2, or that labor productivity in F_1 surpasses that in F_2, or that wage

---

[21] See **New York Times**, January 10, 1967, p. 3; John Randolph article in **Los Angeles Times**, April 2, 1967; Richard L. Clutterbuck, **The Long, Long War** (New York: Praeger, 1966), p. 74.

rates and labor incentives differ in the two firms, or that the speed of delivery or the quality of product differs. Market conditions may not differ at all, or not by enough to explain differences in performance.

In other words, even within the framework of a purely endogenous explanation (in the sense of *conditions within the country* rather than assistance from outside the country), we should make a distinction between factors accounting for R's success which are to be found *within* R itself and factors prevailing within the country but *outside* R.

Thus, endogeny needs to be further subdivided: endogenous with respect to the country, and endogenous with respect to the R movement itself. On this basis, one can accept pure endogeny without accepting the hearts-and-minds view that it is conditions prevailing in the country that explain successful R. It is possible to assert, on the one hand, that the success of R may be determined by factors inside its area of operation, and to deny, on the other, that its fortune depends decisively on the amount of sympathy for R and the extent of deprivation to which the bulk of the population is subjected. In this light, the subject of rebellion and counterrebellion should be considered as much a problem in organization and management as in political-economic development.

A comment very much in this spirit is made by George Kennan. Discussing the Bolshevik revolution's conquest of the Tsarist regime, he observes that the revolution's success depended on

> . . . the extraordinary discipline, compactness and conspiratorial tightness of the Communist Party; the magnificent political leadership . . . [of] Lenin; and the driving, unrelenting military leadership which the Party gave to the Red Army units in the civil war. . . . The cutting edge of these qualities was of far greater effectiveness than any of the shifting, undependable winds of popular sympathy. [22]

The Population Between R and A

The basic importance of the population to R is as a principal— though not exclusive—source of inputs on which the insurgent

[22] **Foreign Affairs,** Vol. 46, No. 1, October, 1967, 7.

system depends. This role is not necessarily less important than that ascribed to it in the hearts-and-minds view, but the role is different. What are some of the differences?

One difference is that the required size of the population that provides the needed inputs can be, as noted earlier, quite small.[23] Depending upon the size of the R system and the stage of its activities, the inputs of food, personnel, weapons, and information that it needs can be more or less limited, and consequently the subset of the population that is involved can be extremely limited. In other words, a small popular minority can be operationally a quite satisfactory underpinning for R, with a generalized impact that may be relatively large.

As a source of inputs, the important characteristic for scrutiny in this minority of the population is behavior or conduct, not sympathies or preferences. Conduct is, of course, affected by both preferences (goals) and opportunities (options). But there are at least two reasons that suggest the analysis of opportunities may be more rewarding than that of preferences. The first is that opportunities are more readily and reliably observable than preferences. Economy of effort would generally warrant seeking explanations that are readily available before looking for those that are elusive. The second reason is that the particular set of preferences to which the behavior of the population is relevant may have relatively little to do with sympathy for, or identification with, either contesting side—the insurgents or the authority. A pervasive, and probably frequent, passivity of feeling toward both sides is quite consonant with popular behavior that is highly beneficial to one side. As we have argued earlier, limiting damage or enhancing gain may be a sufficient explanation for the behavior of the population, without recourse to more elusive explanations concerning putative preferences or sympathies.

According to the alternative approach we are describing, it is appropriate to view an individual or group within the population as a rational decisionmaker who assesses opportunities and consequences of alternative actions.[24] The assessment involves a set of preference functions in which feeling for A or R may be relatively unimportant, or may even take a different direction

---

[23] See Chapter 2, pp. 9-10.

[24] The Appendix to this chapter extends this idealized view of the individual as a rational calculator in the insurgency context.

from that obtained by attributing the burden of explanation for popular behavior to sympathetic feelings alone.

Moreover, the time horizon over which the calculations of this hypothetical and rational *decisionmaking* unit extends may be extremely short. The need to avoid today's damage may overwhelm considerations of long-run preference, or cumulative long-run gain, associated with a different course of action. (The time discount for the population, searching for a path to survival between pressures of R and A, may be extremely high.)

As an example of behavior from pure profit-maximization, note the following description by a Viet Cong defector of the reasons for his action:

> Question: What made you decide to rally [that is, defect]?
> Answer: . . . I thought that in fighting on the GVN side, a soldier may be happy because he has a good salary and even though he dies on the battlefield, he dies with a full stomach. On the contrary, a VC soldier usually eats at 3 p.m. a rice bowl as small as that [the subject described it with his fingers] and he walks all night long to fight and to die with an empty stomach.[25]

Or again the following statement by a Viet Cong prisoner (or defector?):

> I do not know which side is winning . . . I did not think about which side was winning. I take the side which can do the most for me.[26]

Frequently, of course, pure profit-maximizing or damage-limiting influences may be less operative than a mixture of the two. For example, both influences may merge when the population is astute enough to comply, or seem to comply, with *both* A and R. Thus, in the Philippines during the Aguinaldo rebellion, a picture of jointly compliant behavior emerges in the following account by General Adna Chaffee:

> Throughout these islands, wherever a *presidente* of a *pueblo* or *cabeza* of a *barrio* was appointed or elected

[25] From a series of RAND interviews with former Viet Cong members.
[26] **Ibid.**

under American authority, he, with few exceptions . . .
acted in the same capacity for the insurgents. . . . This
dual form of government existed everywhere, in strongly
garrisoned towns like Manila and in the smallest *barrio*.
. . . [They] now commenced the difficult task of serving
two masters. In all lawful matters, they served with due
appearance of loyalty to the American government,
while at the same time . . . they secretly levied and collected taxes . . . from the people. . . . They held communications with the enemy, and in all ways open to
them gave the guerrilla bands aid and comfort.[27]

Notwithstanding the earlier point about the high time discount for the population and the probably overriding necessity
of choosing today's safety at the cost of tomorrow's welfare, there
is presumably a negative correlation between a population's belief in the eventual victory of a particular side (whether A or R)
and the level of immediate threat required from that side to obtain a given degree of compliance. If I expect a particular side to
lose—that is, myself to be ultimately at the mercy of its enemy—
I will need a higher instant threat to offset the forecast of future
damage at the hands of the other side.

Note that in the preceding discussion of the importance of
profit-maximizing—in both the pure- and mixed-motivation
examples—there would appear to be an inconsistency with the
earlier discussion of the limited effectiveness of raising income
and alleviating deprivation in securing compliant behavior. Resolution of the apparent inconsistency can be put in the following
terms: considerations of gain have a more certain effect on income than on preferences; to the extent that a given side can
manage the rate of exchange between gains and compliant behavior—that is, the substitution effect—its access to compliance is
likely to be enhanced. But if the terms of exchange are not manipulated at the same time as income is raised, the benefactor
may very well be himself adversely affected by the benefits he is
providing, which may redound instead to the advantage of the
other side.[28]

To recapitulate the main points of contrast between the role
of the population in the approach we have been describing and

[27] Quoted by Leon Wolff in **Little Brown Brother** (Garden City: Doubleday, 1961), p. 334.
[28] See the Appendix to Chapter 2.

its role in the hearts-and-minds view, let us set down four principal points:

1. As a source of critical inputs needed by R in its growth and progress, the proportion of the population that is important can be a small minority, rather than a plurality or majority.
2. In discussing the population, emphasis should be placed on behavior, rather than on attitudes and sympathies. Attitudes, in the sense of preferences, affect behavior but are not identical with it; nor in most cases are they the primary influence on it.
3. In addition to attitudes and feelings, what influences behavior are the opportunities available to the population for choosing. In the population's calculations of the options available, *predictions* of the consequences of alternative actions may be crucial. Such predictions determine the estimates of profit (gain) or damage (loss) which influence behavior.
4. Moreover, the predictions within which profit-maximizing or damage-limiting calculations are made are very likely to give heavy weight to short-term as against long-term prospects—that is, to be accompanied by a high implicit time discount.

On each of these four points, the message usually conveyed by the hearts-and-minds view is distinctly different from, if not opposite to, that which we have been advancing. To be sure, our approach does not deny that there are those within R and A (and in the population, generally) who are disposed to disregard personal considerations on behalf of loyalty to a cause. Often R has an edge over A in this respect. But frequently feelings about a cause begin to merge with calculations of gain and loss. And where dissonance between them arises and endures, the result is often a change of feelings, rather than acceptance of repeated loss.

Appendix to Chapter 3

Cost-Benefit Calculations and Behavior

The demand and supply formulation can also be described in terms of the costs and benefits of rebellion, as the population views them. Consider the following diagram in which costs (as calculated by an individual or group) are measured vertically, benefits horizontally.[1]

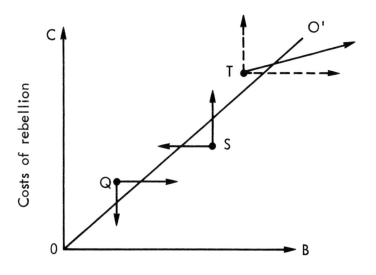

Benefits of rebellion

For all points lying along OO', costs and benefits are equal. For A, the desirable region is above OO', for R below OO'. At any given time, an individual's calculations may locate him at a particular point in the field. For example, an individual at Q is a

---

[1] We assume (conveniently) that nonmaterial and probabilistic elements in benefits and costs can be handled through a Von Neumann-Morgenstern decision-theoretic process that individuals in the population engage in, or simulate in an approximate way. Cf. Howard R. Raiffa, **Decision Analysis** (Reading, Mass.: Addison-Wesley, 1968).

supporter of A; or, more accurately, a nonsupporter of R. Toward such an individual, R's objective should be to shift him east or south; conversely, from A's point of view, it is desirable to shift an individual located at S west or north. When both R and A engage in such efforts, it is the resultant that matters. Resultant vectors that are flatter than OO' will tend to strengthen R; those that are steeper will tend to strengthen A. The diagonal vector at T is an example of the former.

In demand-supply terms, eastward (westward) movements represent an upward (downward) shift in demand for R; northward (southward) movements represent increases (decreases) in costs, hence a fall (rise, in the supply of R.[2] Our prior discussion (and some of what follows in Chapter 5, below) suggests that A's efforts are perhaps more likely to be efficiently expended on raising costs than in lowering demand, while R's efforts, with nearly equal likelihood, may be efficiently expended on either. Yet, if concentration on raising costs causes A to overlook R's efforts to raise demand, the resultant may be flatter than OO', to A's disadvantage. Indeed, if R is astute and A clumsy, R may turn A's efforts to raise costs into increased benefits instead. Various examples of this "judo" effect (provoking A to overreact, decoyed reprisals, coercion based on poor (or no) intelligence) are presented in Chapter 6.[3]

---

[2] The cost-benefit formulation can also be related to the discussion of preference effects, substitution effects, and income effects, mentioned in Chapter 2 (see Appendix to Chapter 2). The preference effect represents movements along the horizontal axis (from A's viewpoint, westward movements; from R's, eastward). The substitution effect implies vertical movements (north, from A's viewpoint; south from R's). The income effect may move individuals southward, to R's advantage, because the costs of rebellion relative to income now seem lower than before. Or it may move them northward, to A's advantage, because they fear the loss of their increased income as a result of rebellion.

[3] We are indebted to Daniel Ellsberg for this analogy. See also George K. Tanham and Dennis J. Duncanson, "Some Dilemmas of Countersurgency," **Foreign Affairs** Vol. 48, No. 1, October, 1969, pp. 119-121.

Chapter 4

THE REBELLION'S VIEWPOINT: STRUCTURE, OPERATIONS, AND PROCLIVITIES

Start and Structure

An insurgent organization shares important characteristics with other modern organizations that operate in situations of conflicting interests: large corporations, trade unions, the military services, political parties. Like such organizations, R recruits, trains, and promotes its personnel; obtains and generates information, including information relating to immediate and potential adversaries; locates and procures other inputs that its operations require; raises and allocates funds; and produces and distributes services or products. It carries on these functions, moreover, in an environment of strong interaction between its own decisions and its anticipation of the vulnerabilities, defenses, and countermoves of an adversary. Knowing and preempting the adversary have an important influence on the choices that R makes. Like other organizations, R requires a reticulated structure to perform these functions, and to command and control them.

Yet R has distinctive attributes as well. Its goals include the erosion of existing law, order, and authority; rather than operate within them, it seeks to supplant them with a law, order, and authority of its own. (Of course, R's presumption is that the

48

supplanting order is better than the supplanted one.) R's means are distinguished by a readiness to use violence and terror to accomplish its aims. In this respect, R's distinctive characteristics may be shared by criminal organizations such as the Mafia, outlaw bands of the Western frontier, and the Ku Klux Klan. But its political aims serve to differentiate R from such organizations and place it closer to radical (if more peaceful) political parties.

The operations and proclivities of R, like those of other organizations, are likely to vary with its stage of development and rate of growth. Analysts have variously proposed three or five stages,[1] representing different levels of R's organization and activity. Whichever classification is used, the point is that R is a plural rather than a singular phenomenon, whose operational characteristics vary with its stage of development. An analogy with the process of economic development suggests itself.

One of the standard theories in the economic-development literature concerns the several stages of economic development, the characteristics of each stage, and the values of key parameters that apply there. Rostow, for example, distinguishes a Stage I (traditional society), in which subsistence agriculture is dominant, investment and savings are low, and income is relatively stagnant; a Stage II (the "preconditions" stage), in which preconditions for growth are established in the form of a build-up of infrastructural investment; the beginnings of industry; the creation of a skilled labor supply; a rise in savings and investment; and a more rapid growth in gross national product than in population; and a Stage III (the "take-off" into self-sustaining growth), in which investment and savings rise (to exceed 12 percent of gross national product); industry expands; and national product grows substantially faster than population.[2]

It may be interesting to consider some of the relationships between these stages and the familiar stages in the R literature. One point of interest is that, while attention is given to attitudes, and changes in attitudes that occur over the different stages of

[1] Mao distinguishes a preparatory stage, a stage of guerrilla warfare, and a final stage of mobile warfare. Cf. **Selected Works**, Vol. II, 224 ff.; Vo Nguyen Giap, **op. cit.**, 29-30, 49 ff., 101; George K. Tanham, **op. cit.**, 10-11.

[2] W. W. Rostow, **The Stages of Economic Growth** (Cambridge: Cambridge University Press, 1960), Chapter 2. Rostow proposes two further stages after the development take-off: technological maturity, and high mass-consumption.

economic development, generally the emphasis is placed on changes in key input parameters such as savings, investment, skills, and technology. The same emphasis might be applied to the analysis of insurgency (as we are suggesting in the systems approach discussed here). That is, one might look more closely at changes in key parameters that accompany the launching of R into a self-sustaining phase: for example, the ratio between persons with deep ideological conviction ("true believers") and cadres; between cadres and rank-and-file; between rank-and-file and active and passive supporters; and between supporters and the populace as a whole. Another interesting relationship—also calculable and variable over the various stages of R—is the ratio discussed earlier between endogeny and exogeny. Moreover, some of the same reinforcement phenomena that apply to the successive stages of development also apply to the stages of R. As R manages, with increasing effectiveness, to disrupt law and order and undermine the functions of A, it becomes easier for R to acquire inputs (recruits, funds,[3] intelligence), which in turn increases the effectiveness of R's efforts to undermine the functions of A. A self-sustaining R—where the ratio of endogeny to exogeny approaches infinity—is the result.

Pursuing the analogy further, there may be a high correlation between parametric changes that accompany movement toward higher stages of economic development and those that accompany movement toward higher stages of insurgency. While environmental characteristics of less developed countries facilitate R, as noted earlier, the process of economic and social change in that environment may, within a certain range, contribute further to R's growth. A more skilled labor force, particularly if unemployed, may ease the recruitment and training of cadres. Growth of income may widen R's potential tax base. Development and technological progress may lead to increased unemployment for certain kinds of labor (rural as well as urban), to urban congestion, and to an intensification of frictions and tensions that make R's tasks easier and strain A's limited capacity to take preventive or countervailing action. Contrary to the

[3] Some of R's inputs may be obtained by sales of its outputs. During the spring of 1968, posters produced in the "occupied" **Ecole des Beaux-Arts** of Paris were quickly marketable at attractive prices in New York. While most of the stock was allotted for fund-raising at home, a fraction was devoted to fund-raising abroad: endogeny and exogeny need not be far apart.

usual belief, stages of development and stages of insurgency may therefore be positively associated with one another over a considerable range.[4]

It is important to distinguish the different stages of R, because the problems encountered in each—both from R's standpoint and from A's—are different. Indeed, the distinction between tactical nuclear war and conventional war is hardly greater than the distinction between an embryonic and a matured insurgency: between one in a formative stage, where the population is being organized, training and recruitment are underway, occasional acts of violence take place, and challenge to the established order is beginning; and one in an advanced stage, where the insurgent civil and military organization is already strong, guerrilla operations in small units are underway, and mobile warfare in larger units has begun.

Consequently, optimal strategies for counterrebellion are likely to vary with the stage R has reached. For example, R's selection of targets for coercion and persuasion is likely to depend on its level of development (one possible selection rule: target the "bad" early, the "good" later). On A's part, the relative importance of information and intelligence, compared with firepower and mobility, is also likely to vary with the stage of R's development, as we shall discuss later.[5]

Like other organizations, R starts small. Its long-term objectives are large, but its hard core of entrepreneurs and managers is small, and its initial program of preparation and activity is limited. At the start, it may face competition from other potential revolutionary movements (for example, Castro's initially competitive relationship with the Communist Party and other dissident groups in Cuba).[6] To pursue the economic analogy further, one might regard this competition as similar to that faced by a new firm from other firms in the same industry, as

[4]Although probably **not** at the higher stages of development. Cf. Chapter 7, pp.

[5]Concerning the point about R's activity in selecting targets and combining coercion and persuasion, see Chapter 4, pp.   , and Chapter 6. Concerning the information-firepower-mobility tradeoff question, see Chapter 7.

[6]For accounts of this relationship, see Theodore Draper's **Castro's Revolution: Myths and Realities** (New York: Praeger, 1962), pp. 201-211; and his **Castroism: Theory and Practice** (New York: Praeger, 1965), pp. 39, 81-82. See also Albert and Roberta Wohlstetter, **Controlling the Risks in Cuba,** Adelphi Papers, No. 17, London, Institute for Strategic Studies, April, 1965.

suggested earlier.[7] As it develops, R is likely to encounter, besides competition from the *same* side of the "market," opposition from *the other* side of the market: from A, depending on the
sensitivity and effectiveness of A's detection system in the early
stages of R's activities. Again, one may liken A's opposition to
an emerging R to the opposition that a new firm encounters from
trade unions or existing firms, which may raise the new firm's
costs, or from uninterested consumers, who may resist the new
firm's product.

Thus, an emerging R must surmount competition and opposition to achieve exclusiveness, or it may stagnate or regress
toward failure. The analogous aim for the emergent firm is to
achieve high profits, and if possible dominance, in the industry
within the constraints of the antitrust laws—which is to say, as
large a share of the market as is profitable and as the laws allow.

If one views insurgency in the terms we have been describing, it becomes relevant to ask what can be learned about R by
examining the structure and operations of other organizations.
Recognizing R's distinctive attributes, as well as those it shares,
the organizations that may be particularly instructive to consider
include enterprises that have in common with R a disposition
toward violence and systematic violation of existing laws (although they may, in contrast, lack its dedication to a cause):
criminal organizations such as the Mafia and the Chicago under-
world of the 1920s. Some of our examples will be drawn from
this context, as well as from certain familiar (and less familiar)
rebellions of the past. In the following discussion, we present
propositions about the operating characteristics and tactical
doctrine of R, illustrating them with relevant references, quota-
tions, and experience drawn from both R and non-R contexts.

How Does R Get Started and Grow?

Our basic formulation of R's emergence and growth has
already been presented[8] and needs only brief summary here.
The environment of a typical less developed country [9] provides

[7] See Chapter 3, pp.

[8] See this chapter, and Chapter 3.

[9] For a useful description of a "typical" less-developed-country profile, see
the factor-analysis by Irma Adelman and Cynthia Taft Morris, "Factor Analysis
of the Inter-relationships Between Social-Political Variables and Per Capita Gross
National Product," **Quarterly Journal of Economics,** Vol. 79, No. 4, November,
1965, 555-578.

the market for R. The many deep grievances, frictions, and hostilities that pervade this environment, combined with its social and economic disjointedness and the resources available —including time and effort—for commitment by individuals and groups according to their preferences, determine the *demand* side of the market.[10] The terms on which such basic inputs as people, food, materiel, and information are obtained from various combinations of internal and external sources, and the efficiency with which they are organized and managed for conversion into the R's activities, constitute the *supply* side of the market. The intersection between demand and supply determines R's intensity at any point in time, and changes (shifts) in these factors account for R's development (growth or recession) over time.[11] (It should be evident that while communist management of the supply side of the market is a case that commands the particular attention of U.S. policymakers, in principle, in other contexts, entrepreneurship and management can be provided under auspices other than communism—such as the United States or its allies—perhaps for R within communist countries.)[11]

How Are Targets Selected?

Two aspects of the problem of target selection in the insurgency context should be distinguished: how an external supporter of R (exogeny) selects targets (countries) to encourage and support, and how R itself (endogeny) selects internal targets (individuals or institutions) to attack.

In divided countries such as North Korea and North Vietnam, target selection is simplified by the saliency of the "unliberated" half of the country—that is, by the very fact of division and the tradition of some degree of national unity.[12] But even in such cases, the selection may not be simple. There have, for example, been strong interdependencies between the insurgencies in Laos and South Vietnam. Even if liberation of South Vietnam through a successful R is the goal, how is the allocation of support between the insurgency in Laos and that in South Vietnam determined? In this case, the answer has probably depended to a considerable extent on logistical considerations: the

[10] See Chapter 3, pp. 28-32.

[11] See Chapter 3, pp. 37-38.

[12] Cf. Thomas C. Schelling, **The Strategy of Conflict** (Cambridge: Harvard University Press, 1960), pp. 74 ff.

dependence of successful R in South Vietnam on a reasonably safe access route along the Annamite chain running down the eastern corridor of Laos to South Vietnam. Hence, it was efficient to support the Pathet Lao *before* shifting to the major effort in South Vietnam.

But in other cases, the decision process may be more complex. How valuable is it to the Soviet Union, for example, to increase the chances of a communist government's coming into power in one Latin American country rather than another? What are the chances for an insurgency to succeed in one country rather than another, and how sensitive is this outcome to various levels of external support? Does a potential endogenous movement have to establish its credentials for receiving external support by demonstrating performance in some way? Or does the external sponsor calculate its priority targets more or less independently of demonstrated performance by R? The questions have rarely been asked, probably because they are so hard to answer.

Perhaps the opportunities for emerging insurgencies to bargain one source of external support against another have grown because of fractures among the communist countries: Soviet support may be more readily forthcoming to avoid a possible Chinese monopoly, and vice versa. On the other hand, the extremely high cost of providing support for the communist regime in Cuba, after its acquisition of power, may have reduced the willingness of at least the Soviet Union to be drawn in as a potential source of support for R. Our ignorance of the external targeting process exceeds by a wide margin what we know.

Turning to the process by which R selects targets to attack within a country, we find that the result may be more predictable. In general, an efficient R is likely to start by picking, as targets for violent attack, resented, low-performing officials and landlords. In any set of officials or landlords, some must obviously be less good and more resented than others. There will always be a median performer, and exactly half the remaining officials will be worse. (The definition obviously also applies to municipal officials, policemen, and college administrators in more developed countries; and the same implications follow for targeting in urban and university rebellions.) Choosing the low-performers for attack enhances the probability of acceptance or endorsement by the population and minimizes the probability of denunciation, because the blame for the terror is extenuated by the offensiveness of the target itself. While ends do not necessarily justify means, it is only ends that *can* provide justification—in this case, by explaining the violence in terms of the target's own offensiveness. In some cases, the R may not choose to proceed against such targets itself; instead, it may settle for removing popular fears and compunctions about squaring old accounts. Members of the population may then freely perform the violence intended by the R (as with the "land reforms" in China after 1949 and in North Vietnam in 1956).

As R grows from small to large, and from weak to strong, the level and the quality of targets may rise. Executing a good official, or a generous landlord, may then evoke reactions of acceptance and nondenunciation from the population, not because the act can be extenuated as a deserved punishment, but rather because previous executions by R have excited general awe and fear. And execution of "good" targets later further strengthens R's claims to irresistible power and inevitable victory. Resignation rather than extenuation is then the principal characteristic of the population's response, though, of course, the two attitudes tend to be reinforcing rather than conflicting.

As R grows, it may thus move from the "bad" to the "good" targets, and from the low and relatively inconspicuous to the high and conspicuous targets.[13] In some cases, R may also *start* with an attack on a sector within the established order that is both effective and even relatively close to R's own goals. The aim may be to disrupt an effort that, by its accomplishments, is conceived as presenting the greatest dangers to those who claim favorable developments are not feasible within the existing structure. By all tokens of what is newfangled rather than old fashioned, the recently created campus at Nanterre, northwest of Paris, was one of the most advanced in the West (hence, in the world). It was there that the "Twenty Second of March Movement" arose in 1968, and the functioning of the university was made so difficult as to induce its closure—the occasion for the outbreak of the "May revolution."

[13] See the more extensive discussion of coercion and damage in Chapter 6.

Operating Characteristics: Doctrine, Adaptation, Learning

Despite R's variability over time and place, several general characteristics usually identify its operations, as discussed in the following paragraphs.

Efficiency and Austerity

It is characteristic of R to preach and to practice austerity in individual behavior and efficiency in organizational activity. There is an obvious (though not logically tight) link between an affinity for puritanism in individual behavior and a concern with efficiency in organizational behavior. And both contribute to the belief, within R and the population, that R's victory is inevitable, a belief that, as we have seen, is important in influencing calculations and predictions and enhancing support for R.

As formulated by Nasution:

> A guerrilla must fight with . . . economy . . . he must calculate his gains and losses like a good business-man. [14]

Pressed by penury and spurred by devotion to ultimate goals for which everything else should be but means, R typically rejects the professional military man's, or the romantic revolutionary's, idolatry of certain stances. As noted by Nasution:

> Guerrilla troops . . . should not defend or attack only to be putting up resistance or attacking [for its own sake]. . . . Acts of "letting people see that we are fighting . . ." must be stopped. [15]

This dedication—in doctrine, and frequently in action as well—to the "cost-effectiveness" calculus may come easier in a milieu at the ends of the military spectrum than in the conventional middle. In the conventional middle, innovation in calculus

---

[14] Abdul Harris Nasution, **Fundamentals of Guerrilla Warfare** (New York: Praeger, 1965), p. 21.

[15] Ibid., pp. 39, 223. The second sentence is attributed by Nasution to an officer fighting under his orders during the conflict with the Dutch.

and conduct is not stimulated by sharp breaks in technique or organization, or by acute scarcity of resources (resulting from the typical poverty of R or the overwhelming magnitude of nuclear weapons costs).

In a sense, the initial pressure of inferiority and resource constraints impels R to discover those elementary principles of rationality and efficiency which it took much assistance and analysis, as well as very high weapons costs, to demonstrate to the wealthy establishments operating at either end of the military spectrum. When wealthy establishments regress to small wars, such as Vietnam, their concern for efficiency may undergo a dramatic lapse. Weapons costs are (individually) small, and the adversary seems, at first, to be inferior. Consequently, the spur to efficiency is lost, costs accumulate, and allocative choices are resolved by simply raising budget levels. A "small war," costing $25 billion annually, may be the result. Efficiency in small wars is evidently harder to learn by A's large establishment than by R's small one. Indeed, for R the learning is mandatory.[16]

Resisting Temptations to "Go Conventional"

Still, the efficiency that rebellions espouse as a matter of doctrine and achieve in practice has to be strenuously safeguarded against increasing enticements. As R grows, for example, it is likely to be tempted to accelerate its entrance into the circle of respectable powers by "going conventional." Mao, for example, affirms that it is precisely "during the progress of hostilities [that] guerrillas gradually develop into orthodox forces."[17] To lure R into making the change prematurely may

[16] Cf. Chapter 6, pp. 94-95. The text commentary on efficiency may seem to conflict with certain examples of R's behavior: for example, the continuation of large unit actions by the Viet Cong against the overwhelming firepower of U.S. forces in Vietnam. Perhaps the exception, if it is one, weakens the rule. But it is by no means clear that the example is really an exception. To the extent that such large actions had the effect of diverting U.S. forces from the smaller actions (i.e., the guerrilla war) and from attacking the local infrastructure of the Viet Cong, as well as of raising the intensity of domestic political opposition to the war in the United States, the large unit actions may have been an efficient mode for the Viet Cong to follow, even if the rate of exchange in casualties was unfavorable.

[17] Gen. Samuel B. Griffith, trans., **Mao Tse-tung on Guerrilla Warfare** (New York: Praeger, 1961), p. 42.

be an objective of A, whose advantage in firepower makes this operational mode clearly preferable to it. In a remarkable manual on guerrilla wars written in the late nineteenth century, Major (later General) Charles Callwell observes:

> . . . at times it will be advisable to impress the hostile [guerrilla] forces with the belief that they are confronted by a less formidable opponent than is in fact the case, for it may be the only means of getting them to fight. . . . For general engagements are the object to be aimed at [by A].[18]

A possibly less astute A may seek the same objective not by stealth or deception, but by maneuver. Thus, after the appearance of conventional Viet Minh units in the fall of 1950,

> . . . the major objective which the French . . . [were] pursuing . . . [was] that of being able to maneuver the enemy's . . . regular divisions into a situation where they could be destroyed in one great battle. . . . This . . . search for the set-piece battle became an obsession of the successive French commanders-in-chief in Indochina until the end of the war.[19]

Of course, the temptation for R to go conventional prematurely is one that A abets at some nonnegligible risk to itself. By concentrating its efforts and attention on the set-piece conventional battle, A may divert resources and activities from the smaller-scale, unconventional operations that its success depends on.

Sometimes R succumbs to the temptation to go conventional with effects that are damaging (for example, Giap in the spring of 1951) or even disastrous (the Greek communists in the late 1940s). As General George Grivas recalls:

[18] Charles E. Callwell, **Small Wars: Their Principles and Practice** (London: Her Majesty's Stationery Office, 1899), p. 78. The Callwell book is strikingly modern, dealing with mobility, intelligence, and crop destruction, among other subjects. In the field of insurgency, it is analogous to Alfred Marshall's nineteenth century text on the principles of economics. One important difference is that the analysis of insurgency has not developed much since Callwell's book; his work is still among the best in the field.

[19] Bernard Fall, **Street Without Joy**, 3rd rev. ed., (Harrisburg, Pa.: Stackpole, 1963), p. 102.

> The rebellion . . . started with guerrilla bands op-
> erating over the whole of Greece from Cape Tainaron to
> Macedonia and Thrace. . . . [It] continually gained
> ground . . . [but then], obsessed by the idea that they
> ought to have under their complete control a strip of
> territory where they could set up a Government of
> "Free Greece," they chose an area in the Pindus moun-
> tains where they established a defensive line. There,
> however, their forces sustained a crushing defeat at the
> hands of the infinitely stronger National Army. . . . [20]

The operational requirement that a successful R forego con-
ventionality complements the doctrinal stress on puritanism and
austerity in personal behavior. Thus, to survive and be successful, a rebellion must have the capacity to renounce the lures of
modernity in military means, and even to regress to primitive-
ness—a lesson Rs have had to relearn repeatedly. For example,
note this description of the Philippine rebels of 1899:

> All spring and summer, Aguinaldo toyed with the
> idea of abandoning Luna's concept of head-on, massed
> resistance to the United States. The Filipino could not
> match the American in tactics, marksmanship, artillery,
> naval support, ammunition and rifles; but there was
> another way . . . this was guerrilla warfare. . . . [21]

And again in the spring of 1946, although the Viet Minh
had already created rather large, conventional units in the South,
in the face of the French offensive in the fall and the winter,

> . . . the Viet Minh, renouncing open combat, dissolved
> its divisions and its regiments. . . . [22]

Similarly, the Algerian rebels dissolved their larger units and
operations in response to the French offensives of 1959-1960.
    Again, in Vietnam, after de Lattre defeated him in the north
in the winter and spring of 1951, Giap refused to engage his
conventional units again until the French gave him both a safe

---

[20] A. A. Pallis, trans., **General Grivas on Guerrilla Warfare** (New York: Praeger, 1962), p. 72.

[21] Wolff, **op. cit.**, p. 247.

[22] Philippe Devillers, **Histoire du Viet-Nam de 1940 à 1952** (Paris: Editions du Seuil, 1952), p. 166 Our translation.

and promising opportunity at Dien-Bien-Phu three years later, and perhaps unexpectedly.

Striving for Flexibility

A rebellion of the puritan stamp is apt to shift back and forth between sharply diverging modes, as changing conditions appear to recommend it. One reason for such behavior is the precariousness of R's situation, as noted earlier. Another is its doctrinal fight against the human disposition toward creature worship (veneration of means) at the expense of glorifying God (adoration of the ultimate goal), which is at the ideological core of a modern, puritan-minded R.

R's flexibility and mobility are noted in Callwell's manual:

> Restricted by no precedents, governed by no strategic code, embarrassed by no encumbrances, they come and go at will. . . . The enemy is untrammelled by the shackles which so limit the regular army's freedom of action. And this fact is of great strategical importance. 23

However, Rs are rarely "ten feet tall," and their capacity to acquire and sustain such flexibility may be severely limited. If a high degree of centralization, as is often the case, is combined with a high degree of vulnerability both in the top command and in its downward communications, R's actual stance may be one of protracted rigidity, with belated and abrupt shifts of position. Commenting on the command and control structure in Malaya, for example, one observer recalls:

> The Communist high command convened only about twice a year to map out policy for the entire six-month period to come, and their communications were poor. As a result, the British gained . . . advantage over a considerable period if they could change the situation in such a way as to make the agreed policy inapplicable. [There was] at least one instance where the guerrillas recognized a certain method as bad, but were unable to

---

23 Callwell, **op. cit.**, pp. 64-65.

change it until the next semi-annual meeting of their high command.[24]

In addition to the limits imposed by its imperfect technology of command, communication, and control, R's flexibility may be limited by the need to maintain some visible forward momentum. Thus, the prospect of de-escalating from larger to smaller unit actions in Vietnam, from main-force actions to guerrilla actions and sabotage, is one that the Viet Cong cannot view with relish. However, the hazard presented to R's organization and morale—particularly that of its marginal adherents—by a loss of momentum does not imply that an R once broken cannot be resumed again (as with the Hukbalahap in the Philippines), or that an R cannot be maintained at a low intensity for long (as in Burma since virtually the end of World War II). By subduing its impatience for total power and a new order, R may develop and sustain a consciously prized capacity for protracted conflict, with a slow rate of change in the balance of strength between itself and its enemy, as well as with a tolerance for long pauses, or—though not without hazard—even extended regressions. While it is irremediably inferior to A in total firepower, R may exceed A's staying power—particularly that part supported by a foreign prop. In fact, it is a prideful conviction of its own staying power which offers R a sustaining substitute for traditional victory.

Emphasis on Staying Power Rather than Victory

While no doubt often dreaming of "victory" over its enemy in that word's traditional meaning, R may steel itself to recognize that this is almost certainly beyond its means, and that the pursuit of such an objective might amount to suicide. Thus, commenting on the "Preliminary General Plan of Insurrectionary Action in Cyprus," General Grivas notes:

. . . it should not be supposed that by these means we

---

[24] Brigadier David Leonard Powell-Jones, in **Counterinsurgency: A Symposium**, The RAND Corporation, R-412-ARPA, January, 1963, Santa Monica, Calif., pp. 27-28.

should expect to impose a total defeat on the British forces in Cyprus.[25]

Dien-Bien-Phu is the exception—and even that battle left the enemy with much of his force in the theater, and with a vast potential outside it (without, of course, the will to use the one or the other).

Staying power rather than traditional victory provides R with its main chance. R's aim is to aggravate and exploit its enemy's limited willingness to allocate resources to the fight. The aim is to degrade the cost-effectiveness of A's effort to such an extent, and to so erode A's prospects (particularly as they may relate to support from a foreign source) that withdrawal becomes indicated. Such an outcome is favored, of course, by the familiar prescription that subduing a given effort of the rebels requires A to commit a large multiple effort. [26]

The pattern is familiar from other rebellions at very different times and places. In the Philippine rebellion against the Americans, for example:

> The insurrectos had no hope of winning the war by guerrilla tactics. With their eyes fixed on the political future, when Bryan's victory would bring them . . . deliverance, they played a waiting game.[27]

In the Irish rebellion:

> In the early summer of 1921 . . . the strength of the British forces in Ireland amounted to about 50,000 . . . the Cabinet estimated that the only way to make sure of winning . . . was to raise an additional 100,000. . . . Lloyd George hesitated to call for the 100,000 men needed. . . . [28]

[25] Pallis, **op. cit.**, p. 5. The point is typical of other rebellions as well, for example, the Spanish rebellion: "During more than five years the guerrillas . . . never obtained a complete victory over a French division and exercised no influence on strategic operations with [one] exception. . . . " J. Lucas-Dubreton, **Napoleon devant l'Espagne** (Paris: Librairie Arthème Fayard, 1946), pp. 327-328, Our translation; and the Irish rebellion: "We have not been able to drive the enemy from anything but a fairly good-sized police barracks," according to the Irish Republican Army's Chief-of-Staff after the end of operations. Holt, **op. cit.**, pp. 256-257.

[26] See discussion of force ratios in Chapter 5.

[27] Wolff, **op. cit**, p. 289.

[28] Holt, **op. cit.**, pp. 251-252.

In another situation, R may aim not so much at leading A to consider the cost of combat excessive, as at weakening A in its conflict with another enemy, one more powerful than R. It is the *other* enemy who will defeat A, although he might not be able to do so if the power he confronts were not being reduced by R at the same time. (For example, the resistance in Axis-occupied countries during World War II in relation to the Allies, or that to Napoleon in Spain in relation to Wellington.)

"Playing It Safe": Surprise, Stealth, and Evasion

Linked with its emphasis on austerity, flexibility, and staying power is R's preoccupation with "playing it safe." The rule is to seek or accept contact with the enemy's forces only when you are certain of success.[29]

The doctrine is amplified by Nasution:

> An enemy target of one platoon must be attacked . . . by one company or more, a target of one company must be attacked by one battalion.[30]

Elaborating "the tactics of avoiding strength and striking at weakness," Mao teaches that

> . . . if we do not have a 100 percent guarantee of victory, we should not fight a battle; . . . when the enemy is well armed and his troops numerous and courageous, . . . we have to evade clashes.[31]

And Guevara, for all his reputation for audacity, displays tactical conservatism by noting: "Even though surrounded, a well-dug-in enemy . . . is poor prey."[32]

In its emphasis on "playing it safe," R stresses the strength it acquires through elusiveness. Retreat and withdrawal are not

[29] That there can be a conflict between this goal and that of attriting an adversary, particularly the foreign source of support for A, is evident. Where R's effort is devoted to influencing the calculation of future costs so as to diminish the opponent's staying power, contact with the enemy's forces may be sought in circumstances where "success" is not anticipated.

[30] Nasution, **op. cit.**, p. 45.

[31] Mao, **Basic Tactics**, pp. 54, 56, 69.

[32] Guevara, **op. cit.**, p. 36.

to be avoided; they are in the nature of the struggle. Break off contact immediately—the doctrine runs—when the calculations that led you to engage in it are revealed to have been wrong. Then the prime objective should be instant disengagement, and the only purpose in fighting should be to overcome the enemy's obstruction of the withdrawal.[33] Thus, when a Viet Minh unit was surprised by the French, the French commander:

> . . . realized that the enemy, far from fighting to the death, was trying desperately to buy time to last until the evening in order to withdraw into the nearby hills. . . .[34]

Elusiveness and withdrawal are similarly emphasized in the tactical teaching of Guevara:

> . . . when [guerrilla] troops are encircled by the enemy . . . before darkness, pick out the best escape route. After nightfall, move out with stealth. . . .[35]

Surprise in the offensive is the counterpart to stealth in the defensive. As Mao elaborates the point:

> The peculiar quality of . . . [guerrilla] operations . . . lies entirely in taking the enemy by surprise. . . . A guerrilla unit . . . should think frequently about the ways in which it can appear . . . where the enemy does not expect it. . . . Then, following the principle that "the thunderclap leaves no time to cover one's ears," the unit can strike . . . and vanish . . . without a trace. . . .[36]

Emphasis is thus placed on hit and hide, a precept whose accomplishment is facilitated by the fact that there is a negative relationship between the level of a country's economic development and the time required for reinforcements to arrive.

Retreat, far from being a loss or a humiliation, is, properly used, glorious and rewarding. Success in withdrawing against

[33] Mao, **Basic Tactics**, pp. 83, 120.
[34] Fall, **Street Without Joy**, pp. 151-152.
[35] Guevara, **op. cit.**, pp. 42-43.
[36] Mao, **Basic Tactics**, pp. 85-86.

odds—foiling the enemy's determination to annihilate R there and then—may prove and foster R's sense of strength.[37]   R's weakness becomes its strength, in a sense which the Cheyenne might readily have understood. Although their "highest ideal was war," they took pride in the fact that

> with their camp equipment, women, children, and aged . . . [they] could still show a clean set of heels to the best cavalry in the West.[38]

In such a fashion R may exhaust A by inducing it to futile pursuits, in the process impressing the population with R's superior agility and elusiveness. According to a participant observer describing the Algerian rebels:

> If we go through a village in the daytime, the rebels come there that night. If we camp in one for the night, they are back in it next morning, a few hours after we have left. All they want is to make fools of us and to prove to the Arabs that they can't be caught, and that even an army will never be able to force an engagement on them unless they want it. . . . Meantime the rebels are winning the savage hearts of the people.[39]

Non-attachment to Territory

It is a major tenet of insurgent doctrine that acquisition and retention of territory should not be an overwhelming consideration. As Mao observes:

> To gain territory is no cause for joy, and to lose territory is no cause for sorrow.[40]

Progress is not indicated by location of the "forward edge of the battle area" (FEBA), as in conventional military conflicts. Instead, chunks of real estate are to be regarded with indifference, whether they are small or large, until the end of the struggle

[37] Mao, **Basic Tactics**, pp. 141-142.
[38] Paul Wellman, **Death on the Prairie** (New York: MacMillan, 1934), p. 89.
[39] Pierre Leulliette, **Saint Michael and the Dragon** (New York: Houghton Mifflin, 1964), pp. 24, 64.
[40] Mao, **Basic Tactics**, p. 67.

when the insurgency will get it all. Expressly because territory is everything in the end, it must be nothing along the way. In Nasution's words:

> We are no longer acquainted with back and front . . . our moves are not cognizant of advance and retreat as in former times. . . . Often leaders who do not understand have pointed to it as a sign of weakness if a guerrilla was not able to defend "his" area. . . . [However], in a guerrilla war the enemy is not prevented from entering any area . . . he is lured into such areas that are difficult to pass and that are some distance away, with the purpose of tiring him, lengthening his lines of supply, thus creating opportunities . . . to . . . destroy him.[41]

On the other hand, when R fails to recognize this "basic tenet of guerrilla strategy," in Valeriano's words, the consequences can be severe. When the Huk disregarded the basic tenet

> . . . [it] gave the Japanese their one major success against the Huk in the Philippines, when they launched an attack on the Huk Mount Arayat "redoubt" in 1943. The attack was successful . . . because the Huk foolishly sought to hold their ground.[42]

R's capacity to learn, from experience, the unimportance of real estate is reflected by the sequel to this incident. According to Valeriano:

> The Huk showed how well they had learned their lessons when Philippine [government] troops undertook an almost identical encirclement of Mount Arayat in 1947, with approximately the same number of well-trained troops, but with far more popular support than the Japanese had had. Reporters, ice cream and soft drink vendors, and sightseers accompanied the government troops, and all the while, horse-and-ox-drawn carts driven by guerrilla supporters carried away supplies of the Huk through gaps in the troop lines. . . . It appeared later that more casualties had probably been

---

[41] Nasution, op. cit., pp. 44, 187.
[42] Napoleon D. Valeriano and Charles T. R. Bohannan, Counter-guerrilla Operations: The Philippine Experience (New York: Praeger, 1962), p. 23.

inflicted by government troops on unidentified friendly forces than on the Huk.[43]

The progress of technology has rendered a firm territorial base less valuable to R currently than in past rebellions. Thus, A's massive advantage in total firepower now makes the existence of a firm territorial base undesirable for R, while radio communication makes such a base unnecessary for R's command and control.

As a corollary to the unimportance of territory, retreat becomes magnified in importance as a tactical maneuver in R's operational doctrine. If territory is unimportant, then retreat becomes regularized, plausible, and central in the planning and conduct of operations. In the words of Truong Chinh:

> When we occupy a place, we must always have in mind the moment when we may have to leave it. When we defend a place, we must always have in mind the moment when we may have to abandon it.[44]

So unimportant is territory that R may defer seizing it, even when the opportunity and strength to do so lie at hand, preferring to exploit rather than to expel A, provided R's longer-term interests are thereby enhanced. Indeed, given the differential value that A and R place on territory, symbiotic arrangements between them are possible. A can (temporarily at least) retain territory without being attacked, under the proviso that it, in turn, allow the territory to provide inputs that R requires. As Sir Robert Thompson notes:

> In many district and provincial towns [of South Vietnam], government forces will be unable to go outside the perimeter, and there may even be a local gentlemen's agreement that, if they do not, they will not be attacked. . . . The insurgents do not yet want to capture and hold such towns. They are still a . . . source of

---

[43] Valeriano and Bohannan, **op. cit.,** p. 23.

[44] Truong Chinh, **op. cit.,** p. 189. Guevara asserts the same principle: "No guerrilla leader worthy of the name will neglect the orderly withdrawal of his forces. A withdrawal must be well timed, quick, and permit the recovery of all the wounded, of gear and ammunition. There can be no surprise attack against, or encirclement of, withdrawing forces." Guevara, **op. cit.,** p. 46.

supply while in government hands, and guerrillas do not want to be encumbered with the administrative and defense problems involved[45]

Imposing an "Air Defense" Requirement on A

By remaining flexible, mobile, and territorially unattached, R seeks to impose on its enemy an air defense type of requirement, which will attrite A's resources and resolution. Commenting on general war, rather than insurgency, Secretary McNamara described the air-defense problem in these terms:

> The requirement for air defense is more a function of the number of targets to be defended than of the number of attacking bombers. Since the enemy would not know in advance which targets our bombers would attack, he would have to continue to defend all of the targets. Accordingly, his expenditures for air defense are likely to be about the same regardless of whether we have a relatively small bomber force or a large one.[46]

The statement has its direct analogue in the insurgency context. Thus, T. E. Lawrence noted that if his relatively small numbers of Arab guerrillas were to operate not "as an army attacking with banners displayed" but as "an influence . . . without front or back, drifting about like a gas," they could create exorbitant resource requirements for the defending Turkish forces. According to Lawrence's rough cost-effectiveness analysis, in an area of perhaps 100,000 square miles, the Turks would need 600,000 men to defend against a relatively small Arab guerrilla force, although they possessed at most 100,000 men for the defensive task.[47] Nasution notes the same point:

[45] Sir Robert Thompson, **op. cit.,** pp. 41-42.

[46] Statement of Secretary McNamara read by Deputy Secretary Cyrus R. Vance before the House Armed Services Committee, February 5: **Hearings on Military Posture and H.R. 4016 Before the Committee on Armed Services,** Eighty-ninth Congress, First Session, 1965, p. 203.

[47] See T. E. Lawrence, **Encyclopaedia Britannica** (1950), Vol. X, 951. An air-defense-type calculation can be formulated more precisely by the following simple model suggested by James Hayes: If G is the size of a guerrilla force, V_i the points to be defended by A, and e the relative effectiveness of A's forces compared with those of R, then A requires a total force, F, given by the equation:
$$F = e \ G \backslash \Sigma \ V_i .$$
F is large relative to G, because $\Sigma \ V_i$ is large relative to e.

> We can create disturbances with extremely few
> arms . . . so that the enemy cannot . . . have any sense
> of security. [48]

The Level of Development
and R's Operating Modes

There is an intimate connection between the foregoing tenets
of R's doctrine, and the structural characteristics of less-
developed countries for which the tactical doctrine has been articulated. To be mobile, flexible, unattached to territory, prepared
to retreat, and bent on maximizing staying power, R must retain
a low degree of visibility when it chooses to. It seems likely that
the visibility of insurgent organization and operations varies inversely with the level of economic development. Hence, underdeveloped countries may provide congenial conditions for
propitiating R.

Technology and economic development steadily depress
the overall degree to which successful hiding is feasible: consider
the desert before and after aerial photography, or the night before and after flares, or the jungle before and after defoliation or
before and after land-clearing.

It is worth noting that while visibility generally varies
directly with technology and development, this is not equivalent
to saying that R's visibility in urban areas is necessarily greater
than in rural areas. For example, it was as difficult for the British
to locate the Cypriot guerrillas in the towns as in the moun-
tains.[49] And in Kenya:

> Looking for the enemy in the forest was . . . to seek
> a needle in a haystack: but looking for him in the Re-
> serve . . . was like looking for a needle in a haystack of
> needles. [50]

Without being able to transform in a short time, or even in
a generation, those characteristics of underdeveloped countries

[48] Nasution, **op. cit.,** p. 204. For essentially the same point, see David
Galula, **Counterinsurgency Warfare: Theory and Practice** (New York: Praeger,
1964), p. 11.

[49] Pallis, **op. cit.,** p. 41.

[50] Majdalany, **op. cit.,** p. 163.

that enable R to achieve invisibility, A may find it advantageous to expand facilities and activities that enhance visibility. Lacking time to wait for visibility to emerge as a byproduct of generalized economic and technological development, A may instead concentrate on developing those particular facilities and activities—those attributes of modernity—which extend its knowledge of who is where and when. Thus, for A, at least in the short run, "census" may be of equal or greater worth than "grievance"; photogrammetry may be more important than pharmaceuticals, and protected telecommunications more important than productive agriculture or modern industry, in reducing the invisibility that underdevelopment offers to R.

Chapter 5

THE AUTHORITY'S VIEWPOINT: CONCEPTS AND CONDUCT OF COUNTERREBELLION

Politics and Force in Counterinsurgency

According to a frequent assertion, in successful counterinsurgency politics is primary and force is secondary. In this respect, counterinsurgency is supposed to differ from conventional war, where the order is reversed.

As noted earlier, belief in the primacy of politics over force characterizes the slogans and priorities of the hearts-and-minds view. But advocacy of the primacy of politics is not confined to civilians. Sometimes the views expressed by professional military men also stress the primacy of politics in counterrebellion, although the typical military view would have it otherwise.[1]

---

[1] Despite frequent rhetoric to the contrary, a probably more typical, but not more accurate, military viewpoint was expressed by General Earle G. Wheeler in 1962, **before** he became Chairman of the Joint Chiefs of Staff:

> It is fashionable in some quarters to say that the problems in Southeast Asia are primarily political and economic rather than military. I do not agree. The essence of the problem in Vietnam is military.

Quoted by Alastair Buchan, "Questions about Vietnam," **Encounter**, January, 1968, p. 7. The reason this formulation is no more accurate than the other is that it focuses on **the amount and the priority** of force (the opposing view focuses on **the amount and the priority** of politics). Both views neglect what in our view are the more important questions concerning the **types** of force and politics, as discussed below.

While the view that politics is primary is both frequently expressed and widely accepted, is it true?

One difficulty in answering this question arises from the unclear meaning of "politics" and "force." Tautology often lurks behind such strongly drawn but loosely defined dichotomies, and this is a case in point. Frequently, perhaps usually, the political effectiveness of an A is judged by whether or not an R is suppressed (deterred), while the suppression (deterrence) of rebellion is construed to depend on the political effectiveness of A. Thus, if Magsaysay was indeed successful in suppressing the Huks, he was politically effective (thereby demonstrating the primacy of politics over force), and if Batista was notably *unsuc*cessful in suppressing Castro, it was because of his political ineffectiveness, thereby demonstrating the same point!

However, if an effort is made to define the concepts so that each can be observed *independently* of the other, it is highly questionable whether the commonplace assumption about what is primary and what is secondary is right. If politics is construed as the domain of nonviolence, persuasion, and consensus, and force as the domain of violence, coercion, and constraint, then the biggest contrasts between counterinsurgency and other types of war probably lie *within* these categories, rather than between them. The main differences (and they are significant ones) between counterinsurgency and other wars should probably be put, not in terms of the commonplace view, but in other terms. The *types* of force, and the *types* of political actions that are most relevant in determining outcomes, are likely to differ significantly between counterinsurgency and other wars. Military techniques that work effectively in counterinsurgency are not likely to be effective in other wars, and political techniques and strategies that work in counterinsurgency are likely to differ from those that work in other kinds of wars.

But politics is not necessarily more important in counterrebellion than in conventional wars—particularly, recent and future conventional wars. In its influence on the outcome of the Battle of Britain, for example, Churchill's political ingenuity played as decisive a role as that played by the Royal Air Force. To mobilize (maneuver) the British populace into such intense resolution that compromise became unthinkable was an act of great political dexterity, comparable in its influence on Britain's stamina and the outcome of the war with the military effectiveness of the RAF. The contrast with the role of domestic politics in influencing military outcome in the Battle of France is obvious and notable. The importance of Syngman Rhee's political ingenuity in freeing the North Korean prisoners-of-war in 1953, and thereby influencing the outcome of the Korean war is another case in point.

Moreover, politics does not seem to be less important in contingencies closer to the nuclear end of the spectrum. Thus, in the Suez crisis of 1956 and the Cuban missile crisis of 1962—in both of which nuclear threats arose, with differing degrees of imminence—political maneuvering was singularly important in influencing military outcomes. For example, recall the profound political importance of the militarily almost valueless Jupiter missiles in 1962.

Of course, politics is equally significant in insurgent conflicts. But the ingredients of effective political action are different from those suggested by the previous examples. From A's standpoint, effective politics requires that A demonstrate a growing capacity to govern—by adhering to and enforcing law and order; by maintaining discipline within and between its agencies; and by completing announced programs visibly and expeditiously. Demonstrating competence and acquiring a reputation for effective action constitute A's political task. Political actions that strengthen A are synonymous with political actions that expand A's capacity to absorb and offset harassment from R.[2] Elections, political organizing, governmental probity, and development programs may contribute to this end.

If, on the one hand, politics is important in conflict other than rebellions, so, on the other hand, is the use of force important in rebellions as well as in other wars. Thus, Magsaysay's reorganization of the Philippine Constabulary into smaller, more decentralized, and mobile units, combined with the altered incentive structure created for the Armed Forces of the Philippines to reward effective application of force against the Huks,[3] was not less important in suppressing the Huks than were the *political* moves (for example, the relatively free elec-

[2] See Chapter 3, pp. 37-38, and this chapter, pp. 82-83.

[3] See Wolf, "Insurgency and Counterinsurgency: New Myths and Old Realities," **The Yale Review**, Vol. LVI, No. 2, Winter, 1967, 225-241.

tions of 1953 and reduced corruption in the civil administration) instituted by Magsaysay at the same time.

The military measures, forces, and capabilities that are best suited for counterinsurgency are apt to differ from those that are best suited for other types of contingencies. Thus, if the forces of Asian countries are designed to meet major conventional invasion by China, North Vietnam, or North Korea, or if Latin American forces are designed for hemispheric defense, their capabilities for deterring or meeting insurgent threats may be considerably less (for a given budget) than if they were specifically designed to meet these lower-level threats. A capability to prevent R—that is, a deterrence capability—requires a highly developed intelligence system, enlarged and improved paramilitary and police forces, and expanded engineering and medical units for civic action in remote areas, rather than conventionally armed and trained military units with heavy firepower and armor. A capability to wage effective counterinsurgency warfare—that is, a "war-fighting" capability—is likely to require forces (as does nuclear war) with a high degree of surface mobility, airlift, and aerial reconnaissance, as well as a capacity for operating effectively in small units for long periods of time while retaining good communications with higher-echelon headquarters. On the other hand, forces to meet a major conventional aggression are likely to stress *not* these capabilities, but rather armor, artillery, fighter aircraft, and air defense, as well as highly centralized operations by large, division-level units. And the *use* of forces trained, commanded, and equipped for major conventional contingencies in unconventional, insurgent conflicts is likely to entail both high costs and low effectiveness. The war in Vietnam is the most obvious and glaring example.

Defense capabilities for deterring Rs, as well as for fighting them in their earliest stages, should emphasize police and militia forces rather than military ones. Such forces are apt to be more closely associated with civil than military administration because their primary mission is preserving law and order and protecting the population. Fulfilling these missions depends critically on an intimate knowledge of local happenings, people, and organizations—in other words, on police intelligence, rather than the order-of-battle, counterforce type of intelligence with which the military tends to be preoccupied.[4]

4 Cf. Chapter 7.

Thus, the requirements in an insurgency context for both deterrence and war-fighting capabilities are likely to differ sharply from the requirements for deterring or meeting large-scale conventional aggression. The ingredients of effective force in counterinsurgency are not less important than, just very different from, the ingredients of effective force in other contingencies. A decision to base force structures on one set of contingencies is thus likely to mean reducing capabilities for other contingencies.

In sum, politics typically plays a powerful and often under-valued role in military confrontations at the higher levels of the spectrum, including nuclear as well as conventional contingencies; and the use of force plays a highly important and often undervalued role in lower levels of conflict, including counterinsurgency. The differences between counterinsurgency and other conflicts relate to the content and conduct of political and coercive roles, not to their relative importance. In analyzing and specifying these roles, the systems view of counterinsurgency differs as sharply from the conventional military emphasis on counterforce (attrition) as it does from the hearts-and-minds emphasis on sympathy.

Waging Counterinsurgency

The systems view of counterinsurgency suggests four methods or tasks, which will be elaborated in this chapter.[5] Deterring insurgency, as distinct from waging counterinsurgency, requires attention to the same tasks, though they become more difficult to perform as the level of R's organizations and operations advances. Both political and military functions enter into the performance of each task, in proportions that are likely to reflect the particular division of labor between civilian and military administration prevailing in a particular country as well as the quality of the task in question. The four tasks involve intervention by A at different places in the R system—that is, moving successively down the diagram of R's operations as illustrated in Figure 1, page 35.

---

[5] See also Chapter 3, especially Figure 1.

Reducing R's Resources: Controlling the Supply and Prices of R's Inputs

The central role of controlling the supply of inputs is summarized in a Vietnamese proverb that recalls a celebrated metaphor of Mao's: "Dry the river and catch the fish." The river must be cut off from replenishment by external, as well as internal, sources of supply. To the extent that internal sources (endogeny) operate, the task of control is likely to fall predominantly on the police establishment. To the extent that external sources (exogeny) operate, input control is likely to depend mainly on customs and border-control agencies, and on border surveillance by the military—on the ground as well as in the air.

In the higher stages of R, the contribution of exogeny to R's logistics may be larger, but its importance in supporting R's buildup and operations at lower levels is not negligible. Even though R, in the early guerrilla mode, maintains or reverts to a primitive level of living, it retains an intense need for inputs of certain key resources, such as arms and medicine, and these are most likely to come from external sources.

Barrier devices to insulate a country from external sources of supply to R may become an important ingredient—though a costly one to A—in waging successful counterrebellion.[6] However, the ratio between potential suppliers of R (both external and internal) and members of R is usually very high, and the potential suppliers are widely dispersed. Hence, barriers may be easily circumvented. Concentrating and controlling the endogenous suppliers—the populace—may therefore also be necessary to achieve a satisfactory rate of return from intercepting external support for R. The importance of whether supply lines are protected or vulnerable is suggested by the contrast between the French in Indochina and the British in

[6] The problem of devising efficient barrier systems, through different combinations of barbed wire, lumber, steel and concrete, minefields, seismic and electronic detectors, ground forces and aerial reconnaissance, warrants more attention than it has received in the abundant literature on insurgency. Devising an efficient system is very likely to depend critically on local factors relating to terrain, weather, and the scope and composition of normal border traffic, as well as on political constraints. John Randolph has provided an excellent introduction to this problem in a series of articles in the Los Angeles Times. See Los Angeles Times, April 16, 1967.

Malaya. Whereas the French supply lines (roads) were highly vulnerable to R's ambushes and demolitions, the Malayan R's supply lines (between jungle and villages) were highly vulnerable to A's hamlet control.

Successful resource control by A may divert, and may be intended to divert, R's effort from fighting to "production," thereby reducing R's mobility and increasing its vulnerability. As Lucian Pye noted in commenting on the Malayan insurgency:

> . . . approximately three out of every five people under the party's control have had to devote all their time and energies to the logistical problem; and increasingly in many areas all the people have had to concentrate on getting supplies.[7]

The importance of R's civil organization, apart from its influence on the population's attitudes and calculations, arises from its central role in locating supplies, collecting them, and forwarding them to the end users. So central is this logistic role that one experienced observer has advanced the theorem that as long as the organization remains intact, the rate of regeneration of R's armed forces (with respect to any given level of damage to them) tends toward unity, even for large damage and short time periods:

> The mere killing of insurgents, without the simultaneous destruction of their infrastructure, is a waste of effort because . . . all casualties will be made good by new recruits [sic].[8]

Although the rate at which R can regenerate its forces is high if the organization remains intact, the presumption is that the rate of regeneration of R's organization is low. It is, in other words, easier for R to reproduce forces if the organization is

[7] Lucian Pye, **Lessons from the Malayan Struggle Against Communism,** D/57-2, (Cambridge: Center for International Studies, Massachusetts Institute of Technology, 1957, p. 51.

[8] Thompson, **op. cit.,** p. 116. A milder, but probably more accurate, formulation is also advanced by the same author (p. 119):
. . . 'fix-and-destroy' operations . . . serve only the limited purpose of killing insurgents. They do not destroy their . . . infrastructure. They must, therefore, be regarded as secondary to those operations which are achieving the primary aim [of destroying infrastructure].

intact than to reproduce or repair the organization itself. The proposition has merit if most of those capable and willing to act as entrepreneurs and managers for R already exercise these functions, *or* if the costs of recruiting and training replacements are high. Hence, if those in the organization, or in its key positions, are eliminated, there is limited replacement. Without replacement, there is a weakened organization. Without the organization, the military force becomes ineffective. [9]

In some cases the *timing* of A's actions may have a major influence on an R's access to inputs. In May 1969, the University of California at Berkeley decided to oust student "squatters" from a piece of unused university land they had occupied. The squatters had some sympathizers among the rest of the student body, and when the forceable ouster led to severe and non-selective violence by state and local police, they acquired more. If the University had waited only one month to repossess "People's Park," the student population of the campus would by then have diminished by 80 percent!

In sum, reducing R's access to inputs requires the interdiction of external sources by border surveillance, barriers, or coercive measures applied directly against the external source of supply, and the interdiction of internal sources by control of domestic resources and population. Waging successful counterinsurgency thus requires that attention be devoted to counterproduction efforts (including the next task, degrading R's production efforts), rather than counterforce efforts alone. R's armed forces are not *un*important for A's targeting, but they are *less* important than R's organization and logistic network in reducing R's effectiveness.[10] Of course, the exact mix between targets that is efficient for A to adopt will depend not only on the relative importance of the targets, but also on the cost to A of attacking them. Combining the two considerations is likely to make an optimal strategy one that emphasizes counterproduction rather than counterforce.

---

[9] An interesting corollary is associated with the reversal of these propositions: if R's infrastructure grows, its potential force strength grows by a larger amount.

[10] See pp. 83-84.

Impeding R's Conversion Mechanism: Degrading R's Production Function

A related task of A's counterinsurgency efforts is to reduce R's efficiency in converting acquired inputs into the outputs of the insurgent system. To this end, A can use various measures to reduce the productivity of R's resources, as well as to force R to divert resources from producing offensive operations to more defensive, protective activities. Examples of the first sort are measures that cause R's forces to lose sleep, to be on the move at times and places of A's choosing. Large-scale B-52 attacks on Viet Cong areas have often been credited with this type of impact on enemy operations.

As for the second sort of measures, one way of degrading R's efficiency is by targeting the production mechanism directly —for example, by destroying crops that are relied on to provide food for R's forces. The difficulty of accomplishing this task springs, of course, from having to isolate R from readily available input sources and force it to undertake its own production. Once R has been obliged to start its own production, the production bases themselves become vulnerable to attack. For example, Valeriano notes:

> As they [the Huks] retreated further into the mountains, their food supply depended on what they could produce out of little clearings that they themselves made. . . . We used aircraft to spot these "production bases." We . . . refrained from spraying the production bases with chemicals, as the British did [in Malaya]. We had chemicals available, but we preferred to fly agricultural experts over these areas so they could determine the approximate harvest time; then just before harvest we destroyed these bases by ground action.[11]

The timing of the strike against such intermediate inputs is a matter of some importance if A is to maximize the wastage of

---

[11] A. H. Peterson, G. C. Reinhardt, and E. E. Conger, eds., **Symposium on the Role of Airpower in Counterinsurgency and Unconventional Warfare: The Philippine Huk Campaign,** The RAND Corporation, RM-3652-PR, June, 1963, Santa Monica, Calif., p. 36. Valeriano's account shows an adroit combination of civil technology (that is, agricultural expertise) with military tactics.

R's effort and the consequent degradation of R's production function.

Forcing R to devote more resources to survival can also contribute to degrading the efficiency of its production of militant outputs. As Thompson notes:

> It must be the aim of counterguerrilla forces to compel guerilla forces to expend their money on mere existence.[12]

And according to another observer of the Malayan campaign, the goal of aerial bombing in Malaya was not so much destroying R's units directly as exacting an indirect penalty by keeping them on the move, and thereby causing the expenditure of energy that otherwise would have been available for offensive actions.[13]

Another way of impairing R's efficiency, at once diverting resources and directly lowering productivity, is to attract defectors from R. If defectors can be attracted from (especially) the middle and higher levels in R's organization, the effects in reducing morale, increasing internal conflicts, and increasing R's anxiety and precautions against penetration of its system can be a major impairment to R's production process.[14]

The degradation of R's efficiency involves a combination of instruments and actions by civil as well as military agencies of A. Effective programs for attracting defectors (for example, the Economic Development Corps (EDCOR), in the Philippines, and, though less successful, the Chieu Hoi ["open arms"] program in Vietnam) involve both military pressures and civil inducements: making the life of a guerrilla appear short or hard to bear, and making the option to defect an attractive alternative in terms of employment, income, and status.

---

[12] Thompson, op. cit., p. 116.

[13] Air Commander A. D. J. Garrisson in A. H. Peterson, G. C. Reinhardt, and E. E. Conger, eds., Symposium on the Role of Airpower in Counterinsurgency and Unconventional Warfare: The Malayan Emergency, The RAND Corporation, RM-3651-PR, June, 1963, Santa Monica, Calif., pp. 60-61.

[14] These effects on R's production function can be distinguished from the direct subtraction of outputs that results from attracting defectors. In other words, attracting defectors has the joint effect of degrading R's production function, as well as reducing the outputs of R's system.

Intelligence is, of course, central to all efforts to degrade R's efficiency, whether they divert resources from militancy to subsistence, or directly impair R's productivity.[15] Information about what works and what does not, and who and what are vulnerable to what combination of measures, must be collected and fed back into A's plans and actions.

Reducing R's Forces: Destroying Outputs

The third aspect of counterrebellion is counterforce. The target is not R's inputs or their sources, nor its conversion mechanism. R's forces are targeted directly. This is the traditional military task; it is best understood, most familiar, and most typically preferred by the military. Emphasis on counterforce enables counterrebellion to be most readily related doctrinally to other wars. It is for these reasons the task to which most attention and resources are usually devoted—usually, from A's point of view, inexpediently.

Even though the counterforce task is primarily a military responsibility, there are apt to be important differences between doing it efficiently in the counterinsurgency context and in more conventional military environments. Recalling the point noted earlier, that it is more difficult for R to regenerate middle and higher levels of leadership than rank-and-file forces, it may be more expedient for A to select R's higher leadership as targets than would be the case in other types of conflict (or than it would be for R with respect to A). The underlying assumption here is that there are usually larger gaps in capability between the higher levels of R's leadership and the next level of organizers than there are in A, and that the capacity of the R system to replace these higher levels of organization and management is more limited.

A notable example of the successful targeting of R's leadership is provided by Magsaysay's seizure of a large fraction of the top Huk leadership at a clandestine meeting in Manila in 1951. Good intelligence and swift implementation lay behind the move, resulting in a substantial setback to the movement, and in the increased effectiveness of Magsaysay's further meas-

[15] See Chapter 7.

ures against the Huks.[16] The incident provides an example of an important point: that the top leadership of an R may be relatively more important and perhaps more separable from the rest of the movement than is the leadership in conventional conflicts.

Another contrast between the roles of counterforce in insurgency and other conflicts is that indirect means of acquiring or reducing R's forces are likely to be relatively more important in the insurgency context. Thus, attracting defectors or obtaining information that enables key figures in the R movement to be seized or eliminated may be both more important and more feasible in counterinsurgency than in conventional conflicts. Hence, the design of reward systems for stimulating defection may be of greater importance to A than the expenditure of firepower. Preliminary studies (in both Malaya and the Philippines) of the relative efficiency of acquiring R forces and particularly key leaders or cadres through such indirect means, compared with the expenditure of firepower against R's forces, suggest that the indirect mode produces vastly greater yields.[17]

Reducing the Effectiveness of R's Actions

Whatever A's effectiveness in resource-denial, in degrading R's production of new forces, or in reducing R's forces after production, A can seek to increase its capacity and that of the population to withstand or absorb R's actions. One aspect of enhancing A's absorptive capacity can be likened to "passive defense" in nuclear warfare. This may involve relocating the population and fortifying the new living areas against surprise attacks by R. (The analogy to hardening, dispersal, and evacuation in the nuclear context is evident.) One example of measures to increase A's absorptive capacity is evacuation of the population from the Quang Tri area just below the demilitarized zone in Vietnam so the people would be less vulnerable to Viet Cong attack (and so the area could be declared a free bomb zone for aerial strikes by the United States). The strategic hamlets in Malaya and Vietnam, which entailed hardening, evacuation, and relocation provide another example.

---

16 To some extent, the special importance of top leadership in an insurgency is analogous to the importance of the top dozen or so leaders of the Mafia and other syndicates of organized crime.

17 See Chapter 7.

The Authority's Viewpoint 83

Another aspect of the task of enhancing A's absorptive capacity is more closely analogous to active defense. It involves building up local defense capabilities, usually in the form of constabulary, paramilitary, or militia forces that can hold out defending a fortified hamlet until A's heavier military forces can provide assistance. This active defensive role may be enhanced, in addition, through aerial patrols that maintain round-the-clock surveillance and can apply a heavy concentration of ready firepower in the event of a guerrilla attack. Small aircraft with long loiter times and enough weaponry to counter a light or moderately heavy guerrilla attack effectively may be an important component in this type of active defense system. The main purpose of such an aerial police would be to provide both the symbol and the reality of A's presence and protection, another example of the mixing of civil and military functions in insurgent conflicts.

Of course, the basic requirement for increasing absorptive capacity for R's output is to strengthen A itself: its capacity to be informed, undertake programs, control, protect, punish, and act and react vigorously, quickly, and intelligently. These are the ingredients of nation-building in the less developed countries generally, whether or not they are subjected to insurgent threats or pressure. The tasks of authority-building are manifestly more difficult in an insurgency or a potential insurgency. But this difficult, long-run task can, in turn, be set in motion by progress in the principal components of successful counterinsurgency—itself an intensified form of the larger task of building effective authority in the less developed countries.

Contrasts Between Counterinsurgency and Other Conflicts

While it is, as we have suggested, expedient for A to join closely politics and force—civil and military instruments—in counterinsurgency, this point is hardly a distinguishing one. Still, there are important contrasts between counterinsurgencies and other conflicts as traditionally analyzed and practiced.

Traditionally, wars between As have been waged and analyzed as *counter*force and *pro*-territory, aiming at the destruction of the enemy's forces and the occupation of his territory. Consequently, the location and movement of the "forward edge of the battle area" (FEBA) were viewed as providing a relatively clear indication of success. To a limited extent, what we previously called controlling inputs (for example, economic warfare or pre-emptive buying) and interfering with the conversion of inputs into forces and capabilities (the daytime strategic bombing in World War II) was also pursued in conventional wars. But their roles were minor in the light of the primary counterforce and pro-territory focus of such wars.

On the other hand, counterforce and pro-territory efforts are by no means irrelevant in counterinsurgency wars, particularly in the more advanced stages of R when the insurgency has established military base areas and territorial control. Nevertheless, the difference in emphasis is important. Counterinsurgency is primarily a counterproduction effort, rather than an effort to annihilate forces or acquire territory. The aim of successful counterinsurgency is to counter R's ability to produce and reproduce forces as well as "harden" the structure of government authority so it can withstand R's attacks while the essential counterproduction effort is gaining momentum.

In conventional war, destroying the enemy's forces (counterforce) is a means of acquiring his territory. Destroying his forces and acquiring his territory, in turn, provide the means of coercing the adversary to accept a desired outcome. In counterinsurgency, by contrast, the adversary may have no territory in the earlier and usually critical stages. (Indeed, as noted earlier, to eschew territory, retreat, evaporate, and accept local setbacks are fundamental attributes of R's operating doctrine.) Instead, A's aim should be to attack R's organization, that is, to attack the apparatus by which the forces and outputs of the system are produced. Counterforce is part of the process, but not the most important part. R's military forces are a part of the target system, but not necessarily the major part. In addition, A must target both the population and the exogenous sources of R's support: the former, in order to influence the population's behavior so as to limit the inputs available to R internally; and the latter, in order to restrict external resupply of key inputs.

Force Ratios in Counterinsurgency

An important point of contrast between counterinsurgency

and conventional wars arises in connection with the much discussed "force ratios" between counterinsurgents and insurgents. Sir Robert Thompson has properly characterized much writing on this matter as "nonsense," and "one of the myths of counterinsurgency."[18]

Part of the nonsense arises from the fact that the data are so ambiguous. It is never quite clear what is in the numerator and denominator of the ratios cited. Do they include only active combatants? And what about guerrillas who are only part-time combatants—should they be expressed in terms of some "full-time" equivalents? And should the counterinsurgents include the police, air, and naval patrol forces, or only active ground combat forces?

Although the familiar ratio of ten counterinsurgents to one insurgent has often been cited as prerequisite to successful counterinsurgency, two important qualifications need to be attached to this ratio, apart from the ambiguity (as noted) of the numerator and denominator. First, widely different ratios have prevailed in different insurgencies: the range extends from one or two to one in the Philippines, to twenty or thirty to one in Kenya, and perhaps forty to one in Malaya, at least toward the *end* of the campaign. The second qualification is that the ratio itself is sensitive to the stage in the conflict at which it is computed, and to whether a given ratio comes about by a build-up of the counterinsurgents or by a reduction in the insurgency's ability to produce forces. To the extent that A is successful in its efforts to disrupt R's production mechanism, the ratio will be drastically raised by the decline in R's production capability toward the end of a counterinsurgency effort. A rising ratio brought about by the reduction of R's forces thus has quite a different meaning from (and from A's point of view a more auspicious significance than) one brought about by a rise in counterinsurgent forces.

Still, as noted earlier, an important contrast exists between force ratios in counterinsurgency and in conventional wars. The contrast arises from the fact that where there is a front line in the battle area, the defender generally has a strong advantage, one further strengthened by defensive fortifications. Con-

[18] Thompson, **op. cit.,** p. 48.

sequently, although there are major exceptions—Israel's rout of much larger Arab forces in the six-day war of June 1967 is a striking example—the familiar planning factor of two or three to one in favor of the defender reflects this advantage. Where there is no front line, as in counterinsurgency, this model no longer applies, and it is more appropriate to use an air-defense model. The defender does not know where an attack may come. Hence, even if he is able to keep an advantage by maintaining a high-level alert at each of the targets, there are so many targets to defend that the aggregate force ratio becomes much larger than that of the attacking force.[19]

Putting the problem this way underscores an important influence on the force ratios needed by A. The better A's information about where and when an attack may come, and the shorter his response time [20] (as through aerial surveillance and lift), the smaller the force ratio he needs. Therefore, A's intelligence and information system will play a central role in influencing force ratios.[21]

Moreover, it is probably no less important to stress the *kinds* of forces that A needs than the *numbers*. As noted earlier,[22] A's mobility, weapon training, and communications are likely to be different from, and considerably less expensive on a unit cost basis than, those associated with military forces equipped for fighting large-scale conventional wars.

Indicators of Success in Counterinsurgency

One of the distinguishing characteristics of counterinsurgency is the difficulty and complexity of finding reliable indicators of success. After the fact, it is easy to put things in their places: to say that at such and such a time it became clear that the insurgency was going uphill or downhill, that the force ratios were decidedly moving in the right direction, or that a decisive turn was taken toward A's success or failure. But *during* a counterinsurgency campaign, it is hard to be clear about "winning" and "losing."

[19] See the discussion in Chapter 4, p.
[20] Below some threshold value. Unless the response time is at least quicker than some minimum value, it may make no difference.
[21] See Chapter 7.
[22] See Chapter 4.

The difficulty of identifying reliable indicators of success is related to the previously noted points about the unsuitability of indicators normally used for evaluating success in conventional war: destruction of the enemy's military forces, and acquisition of his territory (that is, casualties, and movement of the FEBA). Counterforce and pro-territory indicators are not appropriate in counterinsurgency.

Neither is measuring the warmth of popular support, and its shift from R to A, a reliable indicator of success, even if we had a good calorimeter for this purpose (which we do not). Genuine popular support in transitional societies is multifaceted and heterogeneous; perhaps more important, it is rare in any durable sense. And when it appears to be most genuine, it is as likely to be a manipulated appearance, as a deep-rooted conviction. (This is not to deny that genuine support is desirable in principle, or that successful manipulation of its appearance is an important quality to cultivate, whether by A or R.) Nevertheless, as we have suggested earlier, Rs or As can wax in the face of popular dislike, and wane in the midst of popular sympathy.

Rather, the difficulty of assessing successes and observing the process of winning and losing in counterinsurgency arises from the four political-military tasks of counterinsurgency previously discussed in this chapter. Observing each task accurately is difficult, and observation is complicated by the possibility that progress in one task may be accompanied by regress in another.

To be confident that the process of winning in counterinsurgency is actively underway, we need to know several things: that R's access to inputs is becoming more difficult (the prices at which inputs are available are rising, and the quantity available is diminishing); that R's organization is experiencing increased difficulties in converting its inputs into insurgent activities (there is growing evidence of lassitude, friction, and misunderstanding within the R organization); that R's forces are being destroyed (and faster than the conversion mechanism is producing new ones); and that A's efforts to strengthen local defensive capabilities (by hardening, relocation, fortification, and the build-up of a responsible and effective police force) are making progress.

That such an assessment is difficult, demanding an active and competent intelligence system, is evident. However, if there is a single indicator that is more reliable than any other it probably is the rate at which middle- and higher-level officers and cadres in R's organization are acquired by A—whether by defection or capture. Given the high regeneration coefficient of the intact infrastructure, this is the crux of R's strength and stamina. Depleting the core of the organization is the aim; acquiring cadres is the key to the core. In both Malaya and the Philippines, this indicator was—retrospectively—a good predictor. And it has never been deceptively high in counterinsurgencies that have been unsuccessful, probably because it is harder to falsify than other indicators.

The selection of appropriate indicators is further complicated by two problems which, though they also operate in conventional conflicts, play a more critical role in insurgent wars. One problem is possible distortions in the actions of members of A as a result of the selection of a particular indicator. If casualties inflicted on R's forces become accepted as an important indicator of success, incentives facing A's personnel are changed. The reporting of R's casualties may be inflated as a result. Or the threshold of reliability for distinguishing R's forces from the general population may be lowered, so that a higher proportion of actual casualties may be imposed on the population than before.

A second problem is that accurate observation of success requires that the indicators relating to R's own behavior be known as well. For example, if one is concerned with judging the process of winning or losing, it would be useful to know how an external sponsor of R might be viewing the same process. If R is concerned with strengthening its control in one part of the country by executing local officials, then combat undertaken by R in other parts of the country may be considered successful even if R's casualties are high, because such combat diverts A's attention and resources from the area in which control by R is being strengthened. The first problem makes concentration on pure counterforce indicators of success unreliable and misleading, and the second makes the use of territorial indicators inapplicable.

Judging the process of counterinsurgency requires, in other words, intimate knowledge of R's organization and of the impact on that organization of various tasks and measures undertaken by A. What A must be after is suppression of R's *capacity* to undertake disruptive acts to some tolerable (to A) level, so that eventually the continued effort and sponsorship of the residual R will not seem worth the costs. When a given package of measures (or costs) undertaken by A buys a greater current and expected future suppression of R's capacity, then the process of winning is underway.

Finally, it is important not to specify an unrealistically high suppression level in concluding that a win has been obtained. The normal level of dacoity, disorder, and illegal activity in less developed countries is usually high. Efforts to establish an unrealistically stringent suppression level may have the effect of vitiating relationships between A and its own external support, turning allies into suspicious and disaffected adversaries.

Chapter 6

INFLICTING DAMAGE

In previous chapters we have attempted to show how the various factors pertinent to the outcome of the struggle between A and R are related to each other. Now we pass from general to partial analysis, to look at conditions, characteristics, and consequences of each of a few types of instruments employed in the conflict. first, in this chapter, force and coercion; then, in Chapter 7: intelligence and information. In both cases, we shall put forward propositions about conduct frequently adopted by R and A, respectively; to be sure, there are instances of R acting in the way we suggest is typical of A, and vice versa. Castro's R was in many ways similar to the A described below, while Castro's A came closer, in many respects, to the R evoked in the pages to follow.

Motives and Sequels

"Hot" Violence Without Calculations

Commenting on the forces of order in Vietnam, a prominent participant-observer recalls:

> There was a constant tendency to mount large-scale operations, which [served] little purpose . . . merely to indicate that something aggressive was being done.[1]

The rebels in question may have thoroughly learned that the

[1] Thompson, **op. cit.,** p. 165.

weak (in firepower) must deny themselves as targets to the strong. But the forces of order may, in calculation or conduct, not always accept the bothersome fact of their opponents' elusiveness. While the professional military will not frivolously *declare* a limitation of interest in what they do to the enemy, still they may, less consciously, come to view their immediate obligation as maintaining a high level of action *on their own part*, without examining whether they thus enhance impact on the particular opponent they are now facing. That is, an advanced armed force may be more oriented (and may not always know it is) toward what would harm an enemy of its own class, rather than toward what would damage inferior military forces. The rebels, under threat of extinction and less burdened with tradition and pride, might find it easier to consider the situation on its merits.

Also, for A, the low risk of *flagrant* failure facilitates raising the scale of operations; in fact,

> the certainty of never running the risk of a clear defeat, such as an equally armed opponent could inflict upon us, enables any military commander to conduct some sort of operation. [2]

And the incentives facing A's forces are likely to leave this temptation weakly opposed, if opposed at all. As long as the most analytic minds in A's military establishment have not yet agreed on the indicators of "winning" and "losing" in this kind of war,[3] field officers may not feel too guilty about fulfilling the professional duty of spending ammunition. As an observer of the war in Algeria notes:

> The armored patrol that scoured the country in the evening had made a rule never to come back without "emptying its magazines." [4]

Such an aspiration may be pursued even at the expense of enunciated firing doctrine. A's forces may have permission to

---

[2] Roger Trinquier, **Modern Warfare** (New York: Praeger, 1964), p. 59.

[3] See Chapter 5.

[4] Jean-Jacques Servan-Schreiber, **Lieutenant in Algeria** (New York: Knopf, 1957), p. 33.

respond copiously if the insurgents fire first, but not to initiate an action that is bound to result in a high ratio of collateral over intended damage. However, if the other side does not oblige— or simply is not present where one suspects it—the destruction upon which A is intent may be wrought anyhow. [5]

Such a penchant for sheer action without regard for ultimate impact may be strengthened by various emotions that one can permit oneself to express in conduct, as long as reliable measures of effectiveness are lacking.

"It is only natural," judges Sir Robert Thompson, that in the trying conditions created by the rebels' refusal to fight according to other books, "troops will begin to lose their temper" —a reaction that their opponents may predict, welcome, and encourage. [6]

The war at large—a demeaning imposition on the forces of order!—may come to be the object of a rage (to be sure, not always a fully conscious one, for obvious reasons) that is least inconveniently taken out on handy rebels, or the proverbial sea in which they presumably swim. If draftees, in particular, are used against rebels ethnically foreign to them, they may come to hate all that involves the rebels, not only (or not so much) because they have had buddies killed, but simply because the war itself, with all its discomforts, sufferings, and dangers, appears to be the other people's fault. Sensing that one's side has no reliable knowledge how the rebels can be defeated makes one even more disposed to concentrate on harming anybody that seems connected with them.

If the rebels are viewed as criminals, any damage they inflict may appear as an atrocity justifying—even requiring—huge retaliation. An observer of the Algerian war recalls about his service as an officer, when approaching a village:

> If the whole line was ordered to advance, more of
> our men might be knocked out, and then nobody could
> prevent their creating havoc in all the houses. [7]

In other words, it is not a legitimate enemy that is hiding there (and he uses illegitimate devices, to boot).

[5] For an instance from the war in Algeria, see Leulliette, **op. cit.**, p. 24.
[6] Thompson, **op. cit.**, p. 34 ff.
[7] Servan-Schreiber, **op. cit.**, p. 41.

Proper retribution wrought against rebels allows for strong sensations to alleviate the boredom of war, in which nothing may be happening for long stretches of time. A conscript in Algeria supposedly told a fellow sufferer:

> As for me, I strike and I kill, because my buddies are being killed and because I am bored to death (*je m'emmerde*) here. . . .[8]

In such trying conditions one may come to depend on regular doses of pleasure from inflicting damage. Frequently there was in Algeria, an observer alleges,

> rivalry for the distribution of the quarry: the only question was who would procure for themselves the pleasure of torturing, the buddies of the soldiers killed in an ambush or those specialized in the safe job of interrogation.[9]

Where the requirement to be "cool" (disciplined) in the act of inflicting damage is weak, the search for pleasure may distort even the application of measures inspired by plausible considerations of utility. "After several rebel chiefs are caught in women's clothes" during the so-called Battle of Algiers, 1956-1957, a former parachutist recalls,

> we make a point of searching Arab women . . . they are inspected from head to foot, more meticulously than the men—it's not hard to imagine in what manner.[10]

Personal feelings may induce those who inflict damage to violate the calculated precepts of their superiors, perhaps with disastrous effect on the enterprise. Thus, the *Organisation de l'Armée Secrète* (OAS) in Algeria, 1961-1962, seems to have failed in large measure because of the refusal by the rank and file to apply the leadership's code on violence. While a great deal was allowed, or even requested, particularly in relation to the European

---

[8] Jacques Tissier, **Le Gâchis** (Paris: Editeurs Francais Réunis, 1960), p. 73. Our translation.
    [9] Robert Bonnaud, **Itineraire** (Paris: Editions de Minuit, 1962), p. 49. Our translation.
    [10] Leulliette, **op. cit.**, p. 284. Our translation.

rebels' French enemies, much was forbidden with regard (for example) to conscripts from the mainland, toward whom the rank and file's feelings were far from tender. An incident in which a French army patrol was killed in an OAS stronghold noticeably reduced the European rebels' chances to secure the complicity, or even the neutrality, of the armed forces.

Harming for a Purpose

In contrast to such casual or passionate conduct by many As stands the puritanical conduct aimed at by R. R is led by a tight organization devoted to a particular leadership and a general cause. Its active members usually have a sense of moving upward, rather than of suffering or being threatened with major losses (which is apt to induce despair and blind infliction of injury). Oriented toward victory and pursuing it in penury, R attempts to offset a lack of resources by a high efficiency in their use. Thus, R may strive to treat the infliction of damage as an instrument for future success rather than for immediate expression or enjoyment[11] —fearing also the dissolving impact of pleasure on skill. As T. E. Lawrence notes about the Arab army:

> The members had to keep always cool, for the excitement of a blood-lust would impair their science.[12]

Rebels, in addition, may obscurely share the contempt that A feels for them, say, on ethnic or class grounds; they may want to show that they are not savage, but civilized, and hence use violence with greater discrimination.

Engaging in violence for reasons other than its presumable contribution to ultimate victory may then appear, to the perfect rebel, to be a serious matter, conduct to which one would feel tempted only in extreme conditions and which may even—or especially—then be a grave sin. Firing impulsively when one's firepower is low and when the shot may furnish the enemy with precious intelligence about one's location (a well-known point from South Vietnam, 1965-1969) is a far from venial mistake in the eyes of the rebel leadership. On the contrary, that leadership

---

[11] See Chapter 4, pp. 56-60.
[12] **Encyclopaedia Brittanica**, Vol. X, 1950, 953.

typically worships coolness in the service of passion, and prides itself on having learned through "study" (a favorite word of the Viet Cong, for example) what efficiency dictates in the particular and changing situation at hand. "The opponents," notes Che Guevara,

> can be distinguished by the character of their fire. The enemy, well-supplied with ammunition, is characterized by impulsive fire in heavy volume. The guerrilla forces, not so favored, will fire sporadically—not one shot more than absolutely necessary.[13]

Thus, when

> once one of our heroes . . . had to use his machine gun for almost five minutes, burst after burst . . . this caused . . . confusion in our forces, because the rhythm of fire led them to believe that this . . . position had fallen to the enemy.[14]

While the Cuban rebellion hardly lived up to this ideal to the degree implied by Guevara, the aspiration he evokes has been influential in many Rs.

Valuing the capacity to make strikes depend on calculations, R may also cultivate the ability to vary its impact on the enemy by a combination of firepower and less rude procedures—for example, negotiation. When the Vietnamese communists were negotiating with the French Government at Dalat shortly after the end of World War II, the leader of the Viet Minh in the South (Nguyen Binh) issued an order to his armed forces (April 19, 1946), to

> support the Dalat conference by a general offensive on all fronts and by sabotaging the agencies of the French sharks.[15]

Indiscriminate Destruction

One may inflict damage for the purpose of annihilation. One

[13] Guevara, **op. cit.,** p. 45.
[14] **Ibid.,** p. 16.
[15] Quoted by Devillers, **op. cit.,** p. 258.

may not desire to leave a residue for coercion: destroying may
be the "final solution." "They are nine million, and we are one,"
ran a popular saying among Europeans in wartime Algeria.
"Everyone of us should kill off nine, and the problem is
solved."[16]

Or one may proceed to annihilate for a given period a fraction of what may be presumed to be one's total target. When in
the fall of 1901 a considerable number of American soldiers were
horribly killed or wounded by Philippine rebels in a certain
province, the U.S. general in charge ordered the area to be transformed into what later was to be called a "free-kill zone," after
the inhabitants' removal into camps. He informed his men:

I want no prisoners. I wish you to kill and to burn;
the more you burn and kill, the better it will please me.

He directed that Samar be converted into "a howling wilder-
ness."[17] Though the motive may have been backward-looking
(retribution), such conduct could be a case of coercion if those
spared are able to draw *practicable* lessons from it as to how
their own destruction may be avoided.[18]

Partial annihilation, intended to convince the target population that one is resolved to go the whole way, may be effective
if one wants to induce flight or staying-out-of-bounds. When
the first Arab village (Dir Yassin) fell to Israeli forces in 1948
and the belief spread (with the assistance of the Arab leadership,
who overestimated the ratio of anger over fear in the response
of its people) that most of the inhabitants had been promptly
killed, this event triggered the flight of the Arabs from Palestine:
a windfall for the Israelis. By killing Muslims at random in the
European quarters of the big cities in Algeria, the OAS aimed
at a separation in space between the two "communities" of the
country. Analogous to the calculations behind some of the
Anglo-American bombing of Germany in the last war, the communists in Malaya intended to make production fall off by having laborers stay away from places of work made perilous, and
leave places of residence (close to the former) also rendered

[16] Morland, Barangé, and Martinez, **Histoire de l'O.A.S.** (Paris: Julliard,
1964), p. 470. Our translation.
[17] See Wolff, **op. cit.**, p. 307.
[18] See this chapter, pp. 103-104.

unsafe. They may have calculated that the balance of strength between themselves and their opponents would be more favorably affected by a decline in rubber production than by their taxing the high total earnings of plantation workers—that inducing "paralysis" and "chaos" was more worthwhile than coercing. In addition, by curtailing the revenue that the British were drawing from Malaya, the communists may have intended to affect their opponents' willingness to continue the battle— which may also have been a calculation behind the "indiscriminate terror" by the *Front de la Libération Nationale* against Europeans in Algeria.

In addition, of course, rendering the situation unbearable for those who cannot or will not leave has as its objective the acceptance of one's demands as, in the target's view, a necessary and sufficient condition for the cessation of their discomforts. When General J. Franklin Bell introduced military law in Batangas, Cebu, and Bohol early in the century, he explained that:

> . . . it is necessary to make the state of war as insupportable as possible . . . by keeping the minds of the people in such a state of anxiety . . . that living under such conditions will soon become unbearable. Little should be said. The less said the better. Let acts, not words, convey the intention.[19]

The total damage inflicted—if one embarks on such a course at all—may then be thought minimized, if the rate of infliction is high, not low. As General Lloyd V. Wheaton suggested early in the century about the Philippine rebels:

> The nearer we approach the methods found necessary by the other nations through centuries of experience in dealing with Asiatics . . . the fewer graves will be made.[20]

Halfway measures between precise coercive acts[21] and "countervalue" campaigns with high levels of destruction per time

[19] Quoted by Wolff, **op. cit.**, p. 349.
[20] Quoted by Wolff, **op. cit.**, p. 350.
[21] See pp. 100-103.

unit may perhaps run greater risks of being both bloody and vain—of stimulating rather than intimidating—than either of these two policies.

Of course, there remains also, in the case of massive infliction (not to speak of extreme levels of destruction which may make the entire target appear doomed), the possibility that the victims will react by supporting the enemies of those who plague them, rather than by being cowed. "Returnees," an observer says about the Viet Cong,

> reported that indoctrination sessions on the armed struggle cited the Malayan insurgency as a case where . . . *indiscriminate* terror . . . failed. "We were told," said one of them, "that in Singapore the rebels on certain days would dynamite every 67th streetcar that passed along a street, the next day it might be every 30th, and so on, but that this hardened the hearts of the people against the rebels." [22]

But then, this device may be adopted in desperation, after other and less risky procedures have proved unavailing, and when one's resources, or standards preclude making it every *third* streetcar.

Demonstrating Capability

"The OAS strikes whom it chooses, when it chooses, and where it chooses," ran a major slogan of the European rebellion in Algeria. Its selection of targets was probably influenced by the intent not only to draw attention to its existence, but also to heighten estimates of its capacity for destruction, and hence of its prospects. Such estimates, needless to say, may contribute to their own verification.

A similar effect may be sought when an R, raising its own level of damage-infliction, foresees and desires that the authorities will respond by taking it (yet) more seriously. Unless the heightened countereffort on behalf of law and order appears

---

[22] Douglas Pike, **Viet Cong: The Organization and Techniques of the National Liberation Front of South Vietnam** (Cambridge: M.I.T. Press, 1966), p. 251. Emphasis added.

to be rapidly and strikingly successful, the impact on estimates may be favorable to the rebels.

Inculcating Compliance

Beyond instilling useful beliefs about the outcome of the conflict, an R may attempt to establish proper habits of obedience to the future government even before its birth, and a spirit of loyalty (the faith may follow the act).

One way of doing this is by starting with small things, but being deadly serious about them. An observer of the Mau Mau in the fall of 1953 reported that

> . . . boycott had been imposed on smoking, the wearing of hats, drinking beer, and the use of buses, and it was more than an African's skin was worth to be caught by Mau Mau in any of these easily detectable activities. [23]

If the Viet Cong insists on taxing buses traveling on the roads it controls, it is probably not only to collect revenue, but also to present itself as an obeyed-government-in-being.

Coercion

How can one, in the formulation of the Chinese proverb, "kill just one and frighten ten thousand others?" One mode is to cow by a combination of ferocity and capriciousness. The intention may be to evoke this reaction on the part of the population: while one will never be completely safe with *that* power, the least unsafe thing to do is to stay on the safe side with regard to its demands. (The capriciousness is intended to reinforce the impression of power, but it must not be *so* massive as to make compliance with demands seem as unsafe as noncompliance.)

Another, and probably more effective, mode for R is to take seriously the cliché that "force is the only language they understand," and to make its force a language—that is, a set of events (signs) related, with not too much variance, to another such set

[23] Majdalany, **op. cit.,** pp. 190-191.

(referents). R may then combine severity and regularity—may be draconian. [24]

As one observer notes:

> The FLN with one killing, would set an example strong enough to scare a large crowd into acquiescence and, once successful, would stop. [25]

What contributes to such an effect will be discussed below.

To be sure, when infliction of damage is justified by its coercive effect, the claim may be wrong and also a cloak for other motives. If during the Algerian war "the forces of order kill prisoners . . . ostensibly . . . because they hope to impede recruitment to the rebels,"[26] one wonders whether this obvious gain was thoughtfully compared with a plausible cost: impeding defection. The covert joke may become a flagrant one, as observed by another eyewitness in the same conflict:

> As we approach, two men flee from a hut. One of them . . . is wounded in the stomach. He is dying. The captain orders that he be left alone: "He should suffer before he croaks, that will teach him to flee."[27]

What contrast to a serious draconian stance, as it is described by a French officer talking about his opponents in Indochina (and probably making them a few—perhaps only a very few—feet taller than they actually were):

> The Viets spill rivers of blood . . . but always according to a precise line. The various penalties . . . are inflicted . . . with a definite aim in mind, and after an analysis of the situation. . . . The peasant . . . comes to

---

[24] When popular discontent was on the increase in Athens around 620 B.C., Dracon, while not proceeding to a reform of the laws:
   . . . met . . . the demand for publication of the laws, in writing, so that men might know . . . what penalties a magistrate or court had the right to impose.
A. R. Burn, **The Lyric Age of Greece** (London: Edward Arnold, 1960), p. 287.

[25] David Galula in **Counterinsurgency: A Symposium**, The RAND Corporation, R-412-ARPA, p. 27.

[26] Bonnard, **op. cit.**, p. 45.

[27] Benoist Rey, **Les Egorgeurs** (Paris: Editions de Minuit, 1961,) p. 57. Our translation.

believe that the Party is . . . omniscient. . . . The man who has a "correct" attitude . . . has nothing to fear. . . . The system of the Viets excludes all surprise. *Every peasant knows what is going to happen to him, he knows in advance the consequences of his attitude, whether he behaves "badly" or "well."* It is this forecast solidly implanted in the brains which is the greatest force of Ho Chi Minh's camp. [28]

The point is to be as implacable (in the case of disobedience) as one is restrained (in that of compliance), having rendered oneself, in the first place, well-informed about who has behaved how. "Above all it is important," explains a French officer analyzing the conduct of his Viet Minh counterpart (a woman), "to administer constantly the proof that there is no violation . . . without heads rolling." Thus:

> once she had ordered a village to cut a road. To be sure, when night fell hundreds of peasants got busy. . . . But around daybreak [they] began to think of the trouble with the Foreign Legion . . . they were getting into. So they began filling up the ditch they had dug a few hours before. [A bit later], dozens of heads rolled. Since then, the Viet Minh securely enjoys the preference of the villagers, who zealously finish off wounded French soldiers.[29]

If both opponents follow similar lines in this regard, what will determine the outcome? It is an obviously crucial question on which extant knowledge or even reflection is meager. Sets of factors conveyed by such words as *resources, appeals,* and *stamina* will presumably then come into their own, in addition to severity and the accuracy of targeting.

The conditions of impunity offered by a draconian system must be such that they impose only a reasonable cost. If the cost of compliance is unreasonably high, even though lower than the extreme penalty threatened for disobedience, the targets' reactions, in feelings and longer-run conduct, are apt to be different from those of the reasonable-cost case. This is "extortion."

A side choosing coercion may genuinely want to convince

[28] Lucien Bodard, **La Guerre d'Indochine: I, l'Enlisement** (Paris: Editions Gallimard, 1963), pp. 445-446. Emphasis added. Our translation.

[29] **Ibid.**, pp. 252-253.

its targets that it knows how to pick out all the guilty ones and only them, even when they are in close collocation with innocents. Recalling how the few obstinate collaborators with the French in the Casbah were liquidated, the head of the FLN's organization for violence in Algiers (Saadi Yacef) describes the end of one such cafe owner by the action of a famous specialist (Ali Lapointe):

> Ali intervened at the head of a small commando. Medjebri and two of his acolytes were the sole targets. At the moment when Ali entered that Muslim cafe, many customers were already present. . . . Ali directed his fire . . . so that only the three condemned men were hit; there was no innocent victim whatsoever.[30]

A draconian side will stress that its policy, in the expression of the Viet Cong, has "two faces": clemency and punishment. It may tend toward indicating that every target, even the worst enemy, always has it within his power, until the very moment of being sanctioned, to limit damage to himself by some known, feasible, and not too costly conduct. The enemy deterred may then also be the enemy changing sides.

A side oriented toward coercion may wish to choose its examples among targets that are liked as little (disliked as much) as possible by the public that is to be influenced. If an unpopular district chief is publicly disemboweled by the Viet Cong, and his family's arms and legs broken, the message to the farmer may not be less impressive, and may perhaps be less revolting, than if the victims were taken from among his own group. And the chance of denunciation (informing) by the population will be reduced by the unpopularity of the target. On the other hand, a side may want to show—probably nearer to the successful completion of its campaign (that is, in the later stages of R)— that nothing will save even the otherwise most popular violator from his due punishment, thus adopting a stance which, the side hopes, is both morally impressive and conducive to prudence.

One step beyond the pure coercion just described, a side may hold targets responsible for the commission or prevention of acts that are neither definitely within, nor clearly outside,

---

[30] Saadi Yacef, **Souvenirs de la Bataille d'Alger** (Paris: René Julliard, 1962), p. 83. Our translation.

their control to perform or to impede. According to a German military order in the occupied Soviet Union:

> In case of sabotage of telephone lines, railway lines, etc., sentries will be posted, selected from the civilian population. In case of repetition, the sentry in whose area the sabotage was committed, will be shot.[31]

The effect may be to keep people on their toes to prevent their heads from being lost. Again, during the German occupation of the Soviet Union:

> In the villages of Byelorussia, it was only rarely that peasants attacked the Germans or German installations at night, and tilled the soil by day. . . . The inhibiting factor was that after such activity had become known in the village and thereby to the Germans, the whole village would probably be wiped out by the Germans. . . . Informers came forward to save the village by surrendering one person.[32]

But there are limits to be kept; perhaps less effective than the severity of the punishment threatened is the feasibility of avoiding it—particularly when the rule in question is an explicit one. According to an observer, a colonel of the South Vietnamese army acting as province chief

> introduced his own land reform campaign. In Vinh Long, families with sons or husbands known to be fighting with the Viet Cong, or to have gone north in 1954 with the Viet Minh, were given three months to get them back. "I take half their land and say to them that if after three months they have not got their men back, I will take their homes and property," he told me. . . . "At the end of that time I give them another three months. If their men are not back then, they go to a concentration camp and lose their property, which we divide up among those who are for us." "How on earth do you expect them to get their relations back from North Vietnam?" I asked. "That's their business," replied the Colonel. "In this province the men who are

---

[31] Quoted by Aubrey Dixon and Otto Heilbrunn, **Communist Guerrilla Warfare** (London: Allen and Unwin, 1954), p. 142.

[32] Herbert Dinerstein, unpublished manuscript, p. 34.

willing to fight for us [and] their families . . . are those who will do well." [33]

But when the feasibility of compliance—crucial for the impact of such conduct, though the colonel does not quite seem to perceive that—appears to be low, as perhaps in this case, does not the demand itself become a mockery, a pretext for damaging which merely adds insult to injury? Still, the effect may also be one of cowing: if they punish me for even what is beyond me, I had at least better do all I can. Or there may be a mixture of both reactions, depending on the magnitudes of various factors: How free does the victim feel to condemn, oppose, or flee the side in question? How does he evaluate the cost and prospects of counteraction?

One further step beyond coercion-by-regularity consists in adding, to a full application of known and practicable norms, a striking but limited unit of damage that is grossly arbitrary. Having robbed their first bank in Liberty, Missouri, with a parsimony of violence, Jesse James' whole band galloped out of town.

> At this moment George Wymore (or Wynmore), a 19-year-old student at the college, was hastening to his class. When the horsemen came thundering down the street towards him, he ran to get into a house. One of the riders wheeled his horse, drew a revolver and fired four times. When he was picked up later, quite dead, it was found that every one of the four shots had taken effect, and any one of them would have been fatal. . . . Jesse . . . wanted to establish . . . a *precedent of deadliness*, so that future towns, when he raided them, would know that he and his gang would kill on the slightest excuse or without excuse. [34]

Here compliance (or noninvolvement) ceases to guarantee impunity, but disobedience still spells punishment. The victim of torture-for-intelligence cannot be sure that the pain will subside if he talks; but he may be rather certain that it will not unless

[33] Denis Warner, **The Last Confucian** (Baltimore: Penguin Books, 1964), p. 31.

[34] Paul I. Wellman, **A Dynasty of Western Outlaws** (Garden City: Doubleday, 1961), pp. 71, 73. Emphasis added.

he does. Threatened with some damage from which there is no protection in any case, the target may be expected to develop a reaction already noted: better avoid all that I can predictably escape! Will he be less or more motivated in this sense than when compliance guarantees impunity? Again, there will be forces working in either direction: one may be stricken by terror in the face of such ferocity, or one may be impelled by rage as well as discouraged by the possible futility of compliance.

Coercion at large, as well as that variant of it called deterrence, requires unceasing effort to produce and maintain a favorable environment.

The serious coercer will strive for ever higher levels of intelligence,[35] aiming at a situation in which inflictions are consonant with norms (whether declared or inferable from conduct) —in which he damages most of the guilty and very few innocents. When it comes to choosing between substantial losses to the latter and a notably incomplete reaction to the former, the aversion against making a mistake will, in a person genuinely oriented toward coercion, be as strong as that against letting a violator enjoy impunity. The coercer disapproves of such practices as the following, from an allegation about Americans fighting Philippine rebels:

> John T. McCutchen, a conservative reporter, told of what usually happened when the body of a mutilated American was found: ". . . a scouting party goes out to the scene of the killing . . . and they proceed to burn the village and kill every native *who looks as if* he had a bolo or a rifle."[36]

To enable itself to act on less uncertain evidence, the A— initially, probably much less well-informed about the rebels than the rebels are about A—must allocate a substantial fraction of its resources to intelligence.[37] This effort, however, may be thought doomed to failure (how does one distinguish the innocent from the guilty in a faceless mass?) or be unnecessary (are the population and the rebels not close to each other?). The

[35] Cf. Chapter 7, pp. 140-141.
[36] Wolff, **op. cit.,** p. 318. Emphasis added.
[37] Cf. Chapter 7.

situation then arising is described by a French officer in Indochina:

> We whites are, after all, lost in the yellow mass as in a fog. We see badly, we divine badly, we are groping. [Hence] the Viets are beating us in the war of atrocities. [38]

Thus R may have the basis of intelligence for correct targeting for massive infliction of extreme damage, while A, lacking that basis, may be incapable of coercion even if it aspired to such practices.

Not only must the coercer arrange to *be informed* about what the coercees do, he must also arrange to *inform them* about what they can expect from him, by warning and setting examples. Here again, effort is required to ensure that the target population be clear as to what precise lesson is to be learned from damage presented in support of a rule. Hence, damage-inflicters may spread the knowledge of their acts in overt ways, difficult to hide—as when the FLN cut off the noses and ears of people who had, say, smoked despite the prohibitions, and now were impressed into service as walking examples. During the Napoleonic war in Spain

> the Spaniard who had helped the Frenchman has his right ear cut off, and bears on his forehead, branded by a red-hot iron, these words: 'Long Live Mina' [a guerrilla leader]. [39]

Intending both to render their new laws familiar and to prove how correct and complete their intelligence is (how omniscient, hence how powerful, hence how destined to victory, hence how worthy of support on all grounds they are), rebels often leave with fresh corpses a summary of detailed charges. In the Irish revolution, which was notable for the rarity of informers,

> many dead bodies, often of Irishmen who had served in the British Army, were found by the roadside, shot by the IRA with a label attached to them bearing the

[38] Bodard, l'Enlisement, op. cit., p. 452.
[39] Lucas-Dubreton, op. cit., p. 346.

words: 'Convicted as a spy. Spies and traitors beware.' [40]

To be sure, nothing prevents A from imitating its enemy. When "Tiger" Tam, Minister of the Interior, wins "the Battle of Saigon" in 1950:

> . . . one finds numerous corpses abandoned in the streets . . . with numerous wounds inflicted by a knife. Attached to them is a paper with the reasons for their condemnation. This is in the usual Viet Minh manner for the execution of "traitors"; but the grounds indicated are quite out of the ordinary. . . . "so-and-so is a communist assassin who has been executed for his crimes." [41]

Being outspoken about extreme damage inflicted may convey disregard for the decent opinions of local mankind, and thus may cow, if it does not do the opposite—but at least an intermediate reaction is less probable. In the case of an organization with a penchant for self-righteousness which it is capable of communicating, proclaimed ferocity may encourage the population to believe that here is the next legitimate authority, quasi-judicial, quite judicious, and very fearsome.

Nontotalitarian authorities, on the other hand, who under the stress of conflict, resort to procedures greatly at variance with their usual standards may be too ashamed and afraid of world opinion to admit what they have done. Instead, they may trust that the population's, if not R's, own media (such as the "Arab Telephone") will bring the news to those to be deterred (which indeed happened, for instance, after the French repression in Setif, in the spring of 1945). Or they may simply prefer to risk wasting the coercion than to have its use publicized and possibly exaggerated.

It is often affirmed that being severe toward the population, or, worse, inflicting considerable amounts of damage on it, does not pay: one is more apt to arouse than intimidate. However that may be, certain characteristics of damaging behavior by either side—apart from the level and sum of damage inflicted—are apt to affect popular reactions.

---

[40] Holt, **op. cit.**, p. 205.
[41] Bodard, **l'Humiliation**, p. 269, Our translation.

1. *Compliance may vary directly with the degree to which the severity of the sanctions inflicted by one side is understandable*—that is, is seen to exist for reasons other than cowing. The population may be out of sympathy with R, but may also appreciate that, given its business, informing merits death. The population may even understand that the rebels, lacking facilities for locking people up and fearful of escapees turning informers, may have to punish severely or not at all. On the other hand, if, say, a minor lack of respect provokes one side to an extreme sanction, this is more likely to be resented in a way that in the long run reduces compliance[42]—unless that side maintains so overwhelming a threat towards its targets that awareness of misdeeds is obliterated from consciousness.

2. *The less complete the enforcement of a rule, by incapacity or discrimination, the lower the compliance*—not only because of the chance of impunity thus provided, but also, again, because of the impression of weakness and injustice thereby generated. To this extent, more damage, suitably allocated, might be better received than less damage randomly imposed.

3. *The less a side*—while insisting, with severe threats, on a certain kind of conduct—*is capable of protecting the compliant population from the other side's making good on its perhaps even severer threats, the more resentment, and in the long run the more resistance, that side is likely to provoke.* When "the peasant has his choice," proposes a participant-observer of As fighting Rs in less developed countries,

> the government must be ruthless. . . . When, however, an area is outside government control . . . the government has no right to be ruthless. [Yet] there was a tendency in Vietnam to get this the wrong way round.[43]

"In the past," recalls an eyewitness-actor about the treatment of the Huks before Magsaysay, "the farmer who gave food to the Huk, however unwillingly, had been treated as . . . [a] supporter of the enemy." With the new policy under which the rebellion was defeated, "the assumption was that if he was . . . in need because of taxes levied on him by the Huk, he was a per-

---

[42] See pp. 119-121, concerning sequels to insults.
[43] Thompson, **op. cit.**, pp. 146-147.

son entitled to help from his government."[44] (However, to what extent would the gain from such a policy be offset by increased compliance with the other side's demands?)

4. *A side* (usually a nontotalitarian A) *may arouse unfavorable reactions among its targets*, reactions well beyond what they might have been *had a given amount of damage been administered in draconian fashion*, if it appears to be not only harsh but unintelligible and unpredictable as well. Its rationale, if such can be fathomed at all, may change erratically. Sharp deviations from the patterns of strong coercion are apt to create in the population a belief in A's incompetence and destructiveness. On the first count, A may appear doomed, contemptible, and hateful (in its weakness, causing misery); on the second, again, hateful and doomed.

"As for myself," a Eurasian officer—lord of a semiautonomous domain in the Mekong Delta during the first war there—explains:

> I destroy the villages which must be destroyed. I kill those who have to be killed. But the French destroy and kill at random because they don't have the necessary information. . . . Of me the farmers say that I am just. But they fear the Expeditionary Corps because its conduct is unforeseeable.[45]

"It is not only their uselessness," says a French officer in Vietnam about the "unjust atrocities" that according to him were common in his army, "which is shocking, but above all the revelation, through them, of lack of discernment." The latter "causes both hate and contempt."[46]—and rage, though it may be inhibited by fear, about being put into a situation where, with the best of will, one is unable to limit damage to oneself to reasonable levels. "The peasants," this officer explains,

> simply can't divine what the Expeditionary Corps is going to do when it appears in a village; it may just as well set everything on fire as distribute medicine.[47]

[44] Valeriano, RM-3652-PR, p. 209.
[45] Bodard, l'**Enlisement**, p. 287.
[46] **Ibid.**, p. 444.
[47] **Ibid.**, p. 446.

An officer recalling the conflict in Algeria notes:

> Two or three times in a row we visited the same
> village, distributing candies . . . pamphlets . . . food and
> medicine. Then, for weeks, we abandoned the village to
> its fate. Or, the day after, we arrived as warriors . . .
> candies changed into grenades, pamphlets into lists of
> suspects, good words into threats. Now, acting on
> intelligence or caprice, we were going to perform
> population control. . . . Somebody looking suspect was
> just out of luck. A passerby, arousing suspicion, ap-
> pearing at the wrong time or place . . . was apt to
> become . . . one "killed while escaping."[48]

While such conduct may cow its targets, it is more likely to
work against compliance, even apart from the bad feelings it
arouses. If those who obey often are penalized while, in other
cases, those who disobey avoid punishment, the case for
damage-limitation is weakened. So it may also be if the combination of much arbitrariness with high overall damage makes one
suspect a campaign aimed at mere annihilation—in the face of
which chances of survival may seem enhanced through resistance.

Reprisal

A side may inflict reprisals against damage done to it, both
for punishment and deterrence—the latter frequently a pretext
for the former, which in turn may cloak vengeance, which, on its
part, may justify pleasure in hurting and wrecking.[49]
While in one major type of reprisal the victims are presumably members of the other side, in another situation—for
instance, when As are impressed with R's dependence on support
by the population—a contiguous (usually in space, but possibly
in time) sector of the population may itself become the target.
After all, it is easily at hand, in contrast to the infuriatingly elusive rebels, and suspect by opportunity as well as by a (not always fully conscious) equation in A's mind between R and the
population.

[48] Philippe Héduy, **Au Lieutenant des Taglaits** (Paris: Editions) de la
Table Ronde, 1960), p. 133 Our translation.
[49] See pp. 90-94.

Hence, "from the moment at which the French army has suffered heavy losses" in an encounter with the Algerian rebels, explains one of them, "the nearest village . . . should be considered as no longer in existence."[50] And in another Algerian episode:

> We pursue them all day from one village to another, in helicopters, in jeeps and on foot, without stopping, for they never stop. As we go along, we set fire to all the [houses] where we find traces of them, and to a few others.[51]

No case is, or can be, made for the assertion that "traces" indicated the continued presence of the notoriously mobile enemy, or for the implicit contention that, had he been present, he had enjoyed complicity from the population whom he was otherwise supposed to "terrorize."

If survivors connected with such reprisals feel a sense of collective responsibility for the initial deed, perhaps because it happened close to them or was committed by members of a group of which they feel a part, and if the reprisal itself is not felt to be disproportionate, such conduct may seem acceptable to the population. But if the first condition is not met, and if it is not clear how the victims could have prevented the initial act at all—or, at any rate, at reasonable cost to themselves—there is little coercion: hardly a lesson to be learned for future conduct. If *any* member of the population may have to pay for *any* participant in an R whose cause has some measure of appeal (in contrast to that of a gang), the R may indeed come to seem to represent the population: one of its cardinal tenets is validated.

In addition, reprisals at random may hit persons whom a side may want to spare, in view of their contributions to its cause, or the shock produced by damage befalling them.

Still, if large enough numbers are killed in this way, random reprisals may be expedient for some time (here again it is the middle road that is apt to be inexpedient), partly because they inhibit the rebels themselves.[52] In 1945 the French, with rebel-

[50]Quoted by Robert Davezies, **Le Front** (Paris: Editions de Minuit, 1959), p. 155.
[51]Leulliette, **op. cit.**, p. 153.
[52]See pp.

lion in Algeria at a low level, reacted to the death of about 100 Europeans by killing about 15,000 Muslims in Setif; it may have worked. In 1955, with rebellion much higher, the French responded to similar damage by killing perhaps 5,000 in Philippeville; it didn't work. Would 50,000 have done it? The figure of 500,000—mentioned at the time on the mainland in oral and popular recommendations—would probably have produced a striking effect for a far from negligible time. But, apart from certain totalitarian regimes during certain periods, the regard for the public on which A depends, as well as its own conscience, may make it choose a middle level of violence, offering even less prospect of effectiveness than the low or high extreme. (Repugnance to the high level of violence on moral grounds is so strong that the mention of its possible effectiveness is largely avoided in public print. Our violation of this taboo makes us liable to being misinterpreted as advocating, retrospectively, the largest number of deaths mentioned in the above example concerning Algeria. We do not. If we were to advise an A having such an option, we should on moral grounds rule out even considering it. That does not change the shape of reality of which we spoke.)

Provocation

One may inflict damage for the purpose of provoking one's opponent to raise his level of counteraction: he will believe it will do him good, but I foresee that it will harm him. (I may be mistaken, and fatally induce him to abandon the ineffectual middle ranges of violence to which he was accustomed for its devastating higher reaches.) In the first half of the sixties, violent actions by rebels in Latin America against civilian governments or against Americans (such as the kidnapping of a U.S. officer in Venezuela) were often suspected of aiming at a local *golpe*, or intervention, by the United States.

When the relations between my opponent and the population are not bad enough, to my taste, I may desire to make my enemy nastier by wounding him harder. Presumably, this was a motive behind the preference of communist elements, in the resistance against the German occupiers during World War II, for killing isolated German soldiers and then disappearing—

confidently expecting that reprisals not only would seem disproportionately large in the population's judgment, but would also make victims far beyond the Party's immediate sphere. In the occupied Soviet Union

> the Germans had issued warnings that any damage to German installations or personnel would be punished by reprisals on the population living in the vicinity of the crime. The partisans would simply kill a German soldier in some safe place, and . . . leave his body in a village street. The Germans almost always . . . retaliated by burning down the village and killing its inhabitants, [though] often it was obvious that the body had been moved, because there was no blood on the ground.[53]

"Along the route of retreat of the paratroops," an observer reports about an episode of the first war in Vietnam,

> "the Viets had planted on bamboo spikes the heads of the soldiers they had killed, like so many milestones. Some of the men went berserk from it, others cried hysterically when they recognized the head of somebody they had known; others just swore softly that they'd kill every Vietnamese they'd find as soon as they got to a Vietnamese village. . . . " They *did* burn down the first Vietnamese village they found.[54]

At the time of the conflict between the Zionists and the British in Palestine, "children in communal settlements were taught a 'spitting drill' to be used against British soldiers with the objective, sometimes achieved, of goading them into incidents."[55]

It may be particularly useful to induce an opponent to kill his own supporters. As the famous Eurasian officer who was operating on the French side in Indochina explains to an observer:

> The French are blind. They fall into all the traps laid by the enemy. Once they discovered the body of one of their men, frightfully tortured, at the entrance to a village. They set fire to the village, having no

[53] Dinerstein, **op. cit.**, p. 39.
[54] Fall, **Street Without Joy**, p. 268.
[55] Christopher Sykes, **Crossroads to Israel** (Cleveland: World, 1965), p. 285.

inkling of the fact that it was pro-French. The Viets had deposited the mutilated corpse there, warning the inhabitants not to touch it.[56]

Apart from modifying preferences, successful provocations may change the outcome of calculations (on limiting damage or maximizing advantages) in a sense welcome to the provoker. For instance, life in the forces of one or the other side may be refused by a villager so long as his normal environment endures, but may be accepted when it is destroyed.

What I want to provoke may not be enchanced pressure by my opponent against my potential allies, but enhanced intervention by a third party against him. One way of doing this is to cause my opponent to inflict such damage on me as will trigger the third party's intervention on my behalf—a calculation sometimes attributed, in another context, to nuclear-minded Frenchmen (interested in reducing the probability of being abandoned by Washington in case of a forward move by Moscow).

Or, I may myself damage what is of value to the third party whose intervention I want to bring about, finding an excuse to do so in the course of fighting my opponent. When the Cuban rebels of 1897 seemed to adopt a policy of burning cane fields owned by Americans, there arose "suspicion that these tactics were designed to coax us into extracting Cuban chestnuts from the Spanish fire."[57]

Should R start off with a bang—which has obvious advantages for its growth—or begin inconspicuously in order to delay A's reaction? Fearing a countervalue response by its opponent, a side (usually R) may abstain from inflicting counterforce damage that would otherwise be indicated—a reaction, as we noted above, contributing to the usefulness to A of *high* reprisal. For example, an American officer who had commanded U.S. Philippine guerrilla forces in central and southern Luzon admitted that

. . . the Japanese, through brutality to the Philippine people, forced us to abandon harassment. We tried various means of keeping them from retaliating

56 Bodard, l'**Enlisement**, p. 287.
57 Wolff, **op. cit.**, p. 39.

against the . . . civilians, but none worked.[58]

Similarly, an observer of the Southern Sudanese rebels in the mid-sixties noted:

> From time to time the Anya-Nya carry out . . . raids on administrative centers; but these have now diminished because the army's policy of massive retaliation has had some success. The rebels have decided that the consequences for the civilian population of the towns are too tragic to make such raids worthwhile.[59]

A similarly prudent behavior may be adopted if a side believes it is better off not to unleash a counterforce *exchange*. "To Jimmy's way of thinking," explains an observer about a Mau Mau general staying put in the jungle,

> he had but to bide his time and build up his food stocks . . . balancing his nuisance value against the effort it would take the Army to move him. The important thing was not to exceed the limit. He had an instinct for correctly interpreting his intelligence, which was good. . . .[60]

The student rebellions of the sixties in the MDCs occurred in conditions in which provocation assumed a major role for both A and R, in view of the following circumstances:
1. The counterforce capability of R with regard to the establishment at large was low.
2. That of A, in relation to R, was high.
3. As long as violations of established rules and inflictions of damage by R were below a certain level (rising as the decade proceeded), they did not appear to justify the crushing counteraction which (2) rendered possible. The evolving pattern came to include intruding upon, molesting and insulting members of A chosen for "confrontation"; inspecting,

[58] Colonel B. L. Anderson in A. H. Peterson, G. C. Reinhardt, and E. E. Conger, eds., **Symposium on the Role of Airpower in Counterinsurgency and Unconventional Warfare: Allied Resistance to the Japanese on Luzon, World War II,** The RAND Corporation, RM-3655-PR, June, 1963, Santa Monica, Calif., p. 27.

[59] **The Economist,** April 23, 1966, p. 348.

[60] Dennis Holman, **Bwana Drum** (London: W. H. Allen, 1964), p. 108.

throwing into disarray and even damaging objects in their offices; "occupying" premises.

4. But making itself suspected of having induced a coronary in a member of A (fatal to the President of Swarthmore, mild to the Dean of Harvard) was already too much for R, and might expediently be followed by cessation or reduction of attack: punishing itself, rather than suffering a retribution it had rendered acceptable, and thus wiping the slate clean with a view to resuming the offensive. Paving stones were an accepted weapon against the forces of order for a month in the Paris of 1968—on condition that they not kill. A single death clearly due to the rebels would have had a significant impact adverse to them.

5. Similarly, had even one rebel then been killed clearly by the defenders of the status quo, they would have incurred a notable disadvantage.

6. Not only was there a high sensitivity to the damage inflicted by A and R, the preoccupation with the human costs of the battle tended to prevail—with the exception of the upper levels of R and A—over interest in its outcome—in contrast, say, to a contest between landowners and peasant rebels aiming at their extinction, where the mutual infliction of extreme damage is apt to be taken for granted. When students confront academic authorities, demands concerning, say, student power or R.O.T.C. are soon likely to take second place to the insistence on, say, amnesty or the enforcement of discipline.

7. In such conditions, it is of major worth for R to provoke A into an inexpediently (for it) high level of "repression." University administrators or "pigs" may act on the sentiments aroused in them when hit by dirty words or substances; autonomously or uncontrollably (not that an *attempt* is always made on higher levels to restrain them) they may counterattack to a measure which splits A itself, and causes its desertion by needed elements of R. This is what happened when the forces of order reacted sharply (though their casualties may not have been below those of their opponents) in the "Battle of the *rue Gay-Lussac*" in Paris, during the night of May 10-11, 1968, inducing the government's capitulation to the rebels a day later.

8. A, in its turn, is equally interested in having R go beyond

those levels or amounts of violating rules and inflicting damage which have come to be accepted as bordering on the permissible. Thus it was noted in Paris, during the spring just recalled, that the police, recurrently, did not use its capability for preventing, at low cost, the assemblage in the streets of large number of its opponents or the construction of barricades by them. It may have preferred—once having incurred the cost mentioned under (5)—offering television audiences repeated spectacles of masses surging through the city and barricades having to be overcome by bulldozers. One month after the first big battle, ordinary folk were still descending from many parts of the city upon the latest battleground to collar the rebels and ask them to stop.

Hitting the Worst—and the Best 61

A side (usually R) may inflict damage for the purpose of arousing positive reactions toward it on the part of those unsympathetic to its victims. The Robin Hoods prefigure their future reign of justice by punishing oppressors and exploiters, employing some of the rituals customary in the established order for the corresponding acts. Helping underprivileged elements in the population to improve their lot in various ways, R may require strength which it can turn against its beneficiaries, now obtaining compliance inspired by the desire to limit damage. That is, first the rebels assist the population's effort to limit damage to itself from A; then, having grown by that campaign, they in turn threaten damage to the population, *unless* . . . The rebels may then begin to deplete the stock, not of the "bad," but of the "good" agents of A: those who are efficient without being obnoxious, and those who achieve unusually good relations with the population. As an observer noted about South Vietnam:

> . . . as early as 1957, the cream of village officialdom had been murdered by the Communists, who had correctly identified this group as a key element in the struggle.62

61 Cf. Chapter 4, pp. 54-55.
62 Fall, **The Two Vietnams**, p. 281.

And in Algeria a participant-observer remarked about the rebels:

> If they have to choose between liquidating a police officer who everyone knows is a monster and liquidating [an officer] who is trying to make contact [with the population], they will pick [the latter] without a moment's hesitation. [63]

Both kinds of targeting will spare agents of A who are neither here nor there. In 1960 in South Vietnam, there was

> . . . a period of . . . terror directed at . . . officials in the countryside who were either unjust administrators or who, by their good example, served the government well . . . the mediocre, those who saw and heard no evil [in the Viet Cong], survived. [64]

Indeed, they were encouraged in the trait that protected them: "the assassination pattern . . . stimulated mediocrity among civil servants"[65] —an effect which the rebels went so far as to foster by explicit, though discreet, suggestions:

> Especially to low-ranking civil servants, the National Liberation Front would convey the idea that it would not harm a Government of Vietnam representative providing he arranged that the programs for which he was responsible were not implemented in any effective way. . . . A civil servant would imagine he could enjoy the best of both worlds: he could perform well enough not to arouse the suspicions of his superior, but not so well as to earn the hostility of the NLF. He might even be in contact with the NLF so as to be certain they understood his position. [66]

Being Generous

Just as an R may seek to please by making itself the secular arm of natural law against a perverted order, it may desire to impress by unexpected generosity—to abstain from inflicting

[63] Servan-Schreiber, **op. cit.,** p. 70.
[64] Warner, **The Last Confucian,** pp. 160-161.
[65] Pike, **op. cit.,** p. 248.
[66] **Ibid.,** pp. 257-258.

expected damage on enemies so as to foster their disaffection from A, or even their conversion to itself. This device is likely, however, to be productive only to the extent that A does not inflict extreme damage on any agent whose loyalty is open to even marginal doubt. If it does not, it may, for instance, be to the rebels' advantage to be nice to prisoners. In 1947, a participant-observer's colleague

> visited a camp in central China where the Nationalists kept five thousand Communist prisoners. "Where were they caught?" he asked the Nationalist general in charge of the camp. "Between you and me, we have no more than ten real Communist soldiers among these prisoners." "Who are the others, then?" "Nationalist soldiers caught and released by the Communists. We don't want them to contaminate our army."[67]

On the other hand, here are the musings of a French officer who has captured an Algerian rebel:

> If I set him free . . . either he mends his ways and will have his throat cut by his brothers . . . or he doesn't, and then, in order to prove that we have not contaminated him, his first gesture will be to cut a throat.[68]

The other side's ferocity may thus counter the device of being humane.

Insulting

Whatever its motive, an act of inflicting injury may also insult the victim, making compliance (if that be desired) less likely. This is especially apt to happen to a side (usually A) associated with ethnic or class strata that hold in contempt the groups with which the other side (ordinarily R) appears to be connected.

The latter's insulting behavior is often a leaning-over-backward against an obscure temptation to accept their superior's sentiments about them. When lower orders maltreat

[67] Galula, **op. cit.,** p. 52.
[68] Quoted by Héduy, **op. cit.,** p. 293.

their betters, they unwittingly acknowledge, through their very rage, the formidable stature of their victims—who may sense this and then find their treatment more bearable.

But the insults heaped upon the injuries administered by masters to their inferiors are likely to express a more serene conviction that the latter are low in all senses of the word; such insults are harder to take "lying down." For instance, in Algiers:

> One day, a sergeant got a bit high and then scoured the neighborhood in a truck, picking up all the Arabs he came across wearing good European clothes—without even bothering to ask for their papers. He came back with his truck completely full. After assembling his captives in the muddy courtyard, he first made them do a few squats and pushups. Then, because he saw they were trying not to get their clothes dirty, he continued with more and more strenuous exercises. "Stand up! Lie down! On your back! On your stomach! Move your legs, your arms, your head . . . " When one would collapse, completely out of breath, a good jab with a bayonet brought him to order again. We were at the windows, laughing, jostling to get a better view.
>
> Since then, it has become an unwritten rule to make a particular search for well-dressed Arabs. Heaven help the suspect caught with a necktie on and with his shoes shined.[69]

Insult may be harder to take than injury: its presence interferes with the determination of conduct by calculations of limiting damage or enhancing gain. The very fact of continuing to calculate in the presence of insult may somehow be associated with the particular loss to be avoided: by taking it lying down (as my tormentor is confident I will), I prove the correctness of his assertions about me. In sharp opposition to this reaction, as noted above, one of the major motives of an R connected with lower groups is precisely to demonstrate the falsity of one's masters' unfavorable conceptions about oneself, just because these conceptions have an obscure and powerful hold on one.

Combining *little* injury with *much* insult is the least expedient combination, where rage is least impeded by pain and

[69] Leulliette, **op. cit.**, pp. 288-289.

fear. It is also one to which nontotalitarian As, as shown by some
of the incidents already noted, are particularly drawn.

Assimilating the Population to the Enemy

If R is associated in A's eyes with inferior ethnic or class
groupings, A may, as noted, find it impracticable to distinguish
between the guilty and the innocent in the faceless mass (or not
useful to do so, if one wants to produce impressive body-counts),
and regard it as sound practice to presume that any member of
the appropriate sector of the population is a rebel. According
to a historian reconstructing the mood of Napoleon's soldiers in
Spain:

> The prevalent opinion in the Army is this: the more
> Spaniards who perish, the fewer enemies we will have.[70]

"Most of my buddies," a conscript reports about Algeria, "were
convinced that all their troubles were the fault of the *bougnoules*.
They wanted to kill as many as they could as soon as feasible, so
as to go home as quickly as possible."[71]

Devices for Compliance

Modes of Threatening and Promising

Enunciating a demand, a side may immediately execute
anticipatory punishment against likely offenders. During the first
war in Vietnam, recalls an observer,

> an agent of a French intelligence service was in the habit
> of taking his 'clients' up in a plane. He'd throw two
> or three out of the plane, and then tell the others: "now
> you'll talk, or suffer the same fate." [72]

Consider a French intelligence officer's comments on the rebel
leadership of the 'Autonomous Zone of Algiers.'

[70] Lucas-Dubreton, **op. cit.,** p. 364.
[71] Tissier, **op. cit.,** p. 57.
[72] Bodard, **op. cit.,** p. 436.

When one or several members of the Council wanted to install themselves in a house in the Casbah, they first sent a team of masons to construct a hiding place there. The masons immediately gathered together the people in the building and told them, in substance: You are soon to receive important personages. You will be responsible for their security with your lives. And sometimes, to indicate that this was no idle threat, a burst of gunfire cut down on the spot the residents who seemed . . . most suspect.[73]

Thus one may relinquish a strict connection between actual conduct and incurred damage for the present, so as to confer maximum credibility on a new and vital connection of that very kind.

Attempting to make a violator desist, a side may acquaint him with his thickening file or with his current classification-for-punishment. In South Vietnam, according to one observer:

. . . village heads are classified according to their cooperation with the Viet-Cong, their non-cooperation with the Viet-Cong and support of the government, or their non-cooperation with both. The Viet-Cong communicate this classification to the individual concerned. He then knows that cooperation with the government gives him a classification . . . sharply decreasing his life expectancy.[74]

(The implicit condition, of course, is that he recognize his actions in what purports to be his record. Intelligence must be good.)

The full execution of a threat may be preceded by a graded series of warnings, perhaps in the guise of symbolic or limited damage recalling vividly what is to come. The Mafia employed a

. . . system of graded warnings from the cutting down of a vine and the maiming of an ass or mule, to the depositing at a man's door of his beheaded dog or a sheep with its throat cut. . . .[75]

The Binh-Xuyen used to

[73] Trinquier, op. cit., p. 15.
[74] James Farmer, Counterinsurgency: Principles and Practices in Viet-Nam, The RAND Corporation, P-3039, December, 1964, Santa Monica, Calif., p. 27.
[75] Norman Lewis, The Honored Society: A Searching Look at the Mafia (New York: Putnam's Sons, 1964), p. 31.

take small pieces from the bodies of those they had kidnapped, which were then sent by parcel post to families
addicted to haggling.[76]

The demands made by an R on the population usually entail, in themselves, only limited loss to the latter. Thus, if the
demands are backed up by extreme threats, the probable loss
from noncompliance may exceed that from obedience, even if
one is aware of a good chance that recalcitrance will remain
unobserved. It then needs a stern and discerning A to balance
the resulting pull toward behavior demanded by the rebels.

A "totalitarian" side is apt to threaten a target with extreme damage not only to itself—damage which it may be willing
to assume but hopes to escape—but also to others closely
connected with the target. The target may believe it has little
right to impose such loss on others, but that it will not avoid
doing so, unless it complies.[77] As recalled by the American
general officer who had commanded U.S.-Philippine forces in the
Islands while they were occupied:

> If there was one informer in a village that the guer-
> rillas contacted for support, information would be
> relayed to the Japanese. They would round up all the
> inhabitants, usually behead the head man or several of
> the leaders, and often burn their homes and destroy
> their crops. This put tremendous pressure on civilians
> to refuse to support us.[78]

Presumably the pressure could be increased even further by
sharpening the specificity and certainty of the opponent's forecast of who will have to pay for his deed and how. A preferred
procedure of the Viet Minh to induce a Vietnamese soldier serving under a French officer in an isolated post to betray it, was to

> . . . have his mother come to tell her son that she would
> die if he did not deliver the post over to the Viet Minh.

[76] Bodard, l'**Humiliation,** p. 125.

[77] See the earlier discussion (pp. 110-112) about reprisals and (pp. 108-110)
about the other side's inhibited, unaffected, or provoking response.

[78] Brigadier General R. W. Volckmann (Ret.), quoted in A. H. Peterson,
G. C. Reinhardt, and E. E. Conger, eds., **Symposium on the Role of Airpower in
Counterinsurgency and Unconventional Warfare: Allied Resistance to the
Japanese on Luzon, World War II,** The RAND Corporation, RM-3655-PR, July,
1963, Santa Monica, Calif., p. 6.

> She would bring with her the order for her execution
> signed by the secretary of the local executive com-
> mittee.[79]

Beyond this there is double blackmail with regard to, say, a
soldier of the other side and his family: threatening each with
damage to the other. Attempting to forestall the use of this
device by its opponent, a side may take potential hostages for
its members out of the other side's reach.[80] As a counterpart to
threats of future damage, a side may encourage forecasts that
the current level of injury which it inflicts will sink if conduct
desired by it is chosen. The population in a "black" or "grey"
area may be stimulated thereby to contribute to a color change
in the direction of white.

Fashions in Compromising

A side may compromise persons by using their concern for
the undoing of a loss that it has itself imposed on them: their
only hope of restitution is made to depend on that side's success.
If the former owner of property confiscated by the rebels wants
payment, the rebels give him bonds, Che Guevara explains—
documents that become " 'bonds of hope' . . . [to] bind old and
new owners to . . . the success of the cause."[81]

Or a side may bestow a gain (say, land) on the population,
expecting that the latter will foresee the undoing of that gain if
the other side succeeds or if disobedience is shown to the be-
stowing side.

Finally, a side can maneuver a target into a situation where
he believes he is threatened by the other side and can minimize
damage by moving toward the side that put him in this spot.
Thus, a side may in effect give a target its name, expecting that

[79] Bodard, l'Enlisement, p. 88.

[80] Thus, in Vietnam in 1954, ". . . the repatriates going North included the
dependents of the hard-core fighters who were ordered to go underground in
the South. . . . The population exchange enabled the hard-core regulars who
stayed behind in the South to engage in mobile warfare, without having to worry
about reprisals against their relatives, who, during the earlier Indochina war,
were often the first victims of their operations." Fall, The Two Vietnams, pp.
358-359.

[81] Guevara, op. cit., p. 31.

he will thereupon calculate, or can be persuaded, to play its game.

One might acquire (or be led to believe that one has acquired) the reputation of being partisan to the side in question by being forced to commit a compromising act ("entrapment"). This may be done by luring a target in search of advantage; he does not fathom that he will soon be concerned only with limiting damage to himself. Or force may be employed against the person to be compromised, as in certain variants of the Viet Cong's drafting and abducting persons for "re-education courses." Or coercion may occur, as in the case of "forced oathing" by the Mau Mau, compromising one with regard to supernatural entities.

But what seems to the interested side to be a compromising act may, because of a countermaneuver on the part of its opponent, turn out otherwise. As the Viet Minh tried to plant its men within the small posts manned largely by Vietnamese, the French multiplied various tasks:

> The chief of the post [usually a French NCO] . . . might submit his recruits to strange tests. For example, he makes them kill Viet Minh prisoners in public. . . . That precaution does not always suffice. The Viets may instruct their men thus: If the French sergeant orders you to kill Party members, do it unhesitatingly. . . . Volunteer for execution! [82]

Instead of forcing the target to perform a compromising act, the interested side may commit one toward him—for example, by treating him surprisingly well, say, if he is a prisoner. One recruitment device of the Viet Cong was

> to release a captured prisoner almost immediately . . . and without any explanation; the soldier returning to his unit would find his officers highly skeptical of his story. . . . He would be treated as . . . [a] spy . . . whereupon the NLF would find him receptive to its recruitment efforts. [83]

[82] Bodard, l'Enlisement, pp. 87-88.
[83] Pike, op. cit., p. 260.

The target's life may be manipulated in more complicated fashion so as to raise the level of threat to him from one's opponent. Having asked villagers whether they receive visits from the other side and having got an (untruthful) "no" for an answer, a side may arrange an ambush near the village which will damage the other side, or at least be noted by them. Thereupon the first side may re-enter the village and say to the villagers (as in the campaign against the Huks):

> You people have been . . . foolish. . . . Our soldiers came here to see if you needed any help. You lied to them. You said there were no Huk here. They knew you lied, and so they waited for the Huk to come. They killed some, and captured some, but others got away. You know what those Huk are thinking now—the ones who got away? They are thinking that somebody here betrayed them.[84]

The villagers, agreeing with this estimate, change sides. "I don't need to kill Viet cadres," the boss of Hué during much of the first war in Vietnam confides to an observer:

> When I suspect somebody . . . I put him into prison on whatever charge, [and] then I release him without apparent reason. Suspected by the Party, he is eager to clear himself by the excellence of his work. I pass false information to him which he transmits to the Viets, who will liquidate him when they find out. If he is valuable, I call him and demonstrate to him that he is irremediably "burned" with his side. I save him by recruiting him. It is thus that I have acquired my best officials.[85]

The Population Under Cross-Fire

The Dominance of Damage-Limiting

As noted earlier, the effort to limit damage may prevail over aspirations to better one's condition or act according to one's ideals; the more so, the fiercer and longer the conflict. "The villagers," guesses a French officer in Algeria

[84] Quoted in Valeriano and Bohannon, op. cit., p. 171.
[85] Bodard, l'Humiliation, p. 365.

aren't going to vote for those who build schools for them nor for those who promise independence; they are going to vote for the one who can hold the threat of death over them.[86]

What may be mistaken by a side for an expression of the population's antipathy toward it may simply be fear of the damage foreseen to result from the other side's reacting to the first side's approach (for example, by recruitment in a village). And, as noted earlier,[87] a side may be prepared to recruit persons for rather high levels of participation under duress.

As an analyst observed about the occupied Soviet Union during World War II:

> Even though the peasant knew who was going to win the war, in many cases where the Germans had . . . adequate forces . . . [he] might decide that it was safer to submit to the Germans and be hostile to the Partisans. [Although] he jeopardized his future by working with the Germans, he could not afford the luxury of making long-range estimates. . . . He tried to survive in the immediate future.[88]

That is, as observed before,[89] calculations of damage that may befall one during the conflict may dwarf estimates of injury derived from the combination of a particular war record with a particular war outcome.

Members of the population may desire to stay with one side as long, and only as long, as it is profitable or prudent to do so, veering toward its opponent when assessments against these criteria begin to point in the opposite direction—that is, when a change of rule impends, or day is about to break (night to fall). Or the population may—a frequently noted maneuver —attempt to satisfy both contenders at the same time.[90]

If one can plead with a side that one's compliance with its opponent's demands was due to duress, perhaps the sanction will be lightened or lifted. Hence, if a side does not insist

[86] Héduy, op. cit., p. 267.
[87] See Chapter 2, pp. 11-12.
[88] Dinerstein, op. cit., p. 39.
[89] See Chapter 3, pp. 43-45.
[90] Ibid. Chapter 3.

strongly enough on compliance, one should wait until it does (and probably make it do so by an initial refusal). "One of the first steps," a French officer recalls about his civic action programs in Algeria

> was to open a first-aid station. . . . When the population failed to respond to an invitation to use the station, for fear of being seen making contact with the enemy, it was necessary to resort to forced treatment. Twice a week the battalion doctor would make a tour. . . . Another . . . step was to open, or reopen, schools. Again, parents and children did not respond to the first request for attendance; but on being told that, as of a given date, they would be fined for their childrens' truancy, the parents decide to cooperate.[91]

How Does a Side Make Itself Stronger Toward Those in the Middle?

One limits damage by veering toward (1) the more predictable side, (2) the side imposing a lesser cost on impunity, (3) the more severe side. Preferences with regard to these three "goods"—or to the latter two adjusted for expectations—vary. There are, for instance, those individuals who are little tempted to transgress and are hence mostly interested in a low cost of impunity; those who are much tempted to transgress and are hence interested in a side's severity (mildness); and those who especially dislike uncertainty and are hence interested in a side's predictability.

"Severity" refers, of course, both to the level of threats and enforcement, including the chances of concealment and escape. To be stronger with regard to the population may thus also mean, as we already noted,[92] to be harsher toward it. As recounted by a French paratroopers' chaplain:

> An old Muslim, arrested for having sawed off telegraph poles, explains to a captain who expresses surprise about his deed: "Sir, the French come and tell me: you musn't saw off poles; if you do, you go to prison. I say to myself: I don't want to go to prison, I won't do

---

[91] Galula, R-412-ARPA, p. 77.
[92] See Chapter 2, pp. 12-14.

it. The French leave. At night, the rebel comes and says: saw off the poles from here to there. I answer: no, the French would put me into prison. The rebel tells me: You cut the poles or I cut your throat. I calculate: If I don't cut the poles, he'll surely cut my throat; he has done it to others, in the next village. I prefer going to prison. So, Sir, I cut the poles; you caught me; put me in prison!" [93]

A population beset by both rebels and forces of order may feel there is much to choose, where observers accustomed to less uncomfortable situations fail to perceive the difference. One may strongly prefer a high probability of death to its certainty, if that appears to be one's alternative. We shall surely kill you unless you kill so-and-so, R may say to a person approached. The other side, to be sure, may kill you for doing it. But also, they may not find out, or not find you; even if they do, their legality may enable you to survive.

Or one may choose the side threatening a merciful death against the side promising a painful one. "At the time of the last elections," recalls a French officer serving in Algeria

Muslims came to me and said: We are coming to see you, but we shall not vote. If we did, we would have our throats cut. You can kill us with your gun; it's more agreeable to die that way than by the knife. [94]

Reactions to Unintended Damage

So far we have dealt with damage to the population which is intended by a side. But what about the flies who get crushed when elephants fight? On what factors does a population's re-action to collateral damage from the conflict between A and R depend?

Sometimes the population will be hostile to a side in the measure in which that side's fire, though directed at the oppo-nent, makes it suffer. Thus, hostile reactions by moderate student groups against university authorities occurred frequently in the

[93] Louis Delarue, **Avec les Paras du 1er R.E.P. et du 2e R.P./Ma.** (Paris: Nouvelles Editions Latines, 1961), pp. 24-25. Our translation.

[94] Quoted by Claude Dufresnoy, **Des Officiers Parlent** (Paris: Rene Julliard, 1961), p. 124. Our translation.

late nineteen sixties (at Harvard, Columbia and Berkeley), when those authorities called upon the police to oust militant students who had occupied university property, and the police in energetic pursuit of their mission struck against bystanders, as well as occupiers.

But, clearly, rage—and in particular rage against the directly inflicting side—is not the only possible response, as the reaction of occupied Europeans showed during World War II. (Also, if the population's major reaction does conform to the hypothesis previously mentioned, the cost of this to the inflicting side, directly and indirectly, may or may not be higher than the immediate tactical gain from the strikes in question.) In some cases, elements of the population may be sufficiently hostile to the side against which the attacks were intended, to nourish their aversion with this very suffering (as, to some extent, in the situations during World War II previously referred to). Or they may at least be willing to pay a certain—possibly a substantial —price for a preferred outcome of the war. And their reaction is apt to be influenced not only by the amounts of injury produced, but also by their estimate of each side's eagerness and skill in avoiding "unnecessary" damage to the population, directly and indirectly. Once again, ruthlessness, negligence, and clumsiness may be attributed either to the inflicting side or to its opponent who provoked such reactions or gave it no choice; the attributions are, as in the campus disorders noted above, likely to be based on matters of fact, as well as of rumor and sentiment. Finally, the entire dimension of the legitimacy of damage may be dwarfed by the search for, and the execution of, maneuvers to limit it.

If a side imposes a certain conduct on the population for which the other side then punishes it, the population's reaction will depend on a variety of factors: its assessment of the utility of the conduct for the side that imposed it (being much harmed for little is galling); the degree to which that side promised protection from its opponent and yet did not deliver it; the degree to which it assumes some responsibility for the misery it has provoked. These considerations would seem hard to overlook. That they *are* overlooked is suggested by an incident related by an observer of the first war in Vietnam:

Luong-Ha is a Catholic village . . . to the southeast of the Plain of Reeds, at about 20 kilometers from RC-16 [a highway]. It was obeying the Viet Minh peacefully. Then, in Saigon, a program for extending pacification was prepared. And so a column [of the Expeditionary Corps] went to Luong-Ha. The priest and his peasants were drawn in, a militia constituted . . . a post and towers built for defense. Then the column left again, leaving behind it a platoon commanded by a French captain. As a result the village was massacred at night. . . . The Viets immobilized the soldiers by mortar and machine gun fire. They passed between the post and the towers, and killed a good part of the population.

When the French returned shortly afterwards, the vicar reported:

Nobody is working in the fields anymore, nobody is reconstructing his house. The Viet Minh cadre has told us . . . that this was just a warning: next time all the men will be shot. We ask of the French to leave important forces in the village, to send us rice and medicine.

The observer in question (Lucien Bodard) concludes his account of the incident as told to him by the French officer in charge:

But he raised his arms to heaven and remarked to me, "These people are insatiable. I'm not God, after all. I can't put troops everywhere. And I've no budget for rice.[95]

Yet the officer attempted compensation for these incapacities: before leaving the village, he distributed a substantial number of military decorations.[96]

[95] l'Enlisement, pp. 302-305.
[96] Ibid., p. 306.

Chapter 7

INTELLIGENCE AND INFORMATION

Efficient action requires information, as we have stressed before. To this extent R and A face a similar problem. But it is much easier for R to obtain information about A than vice versa. For A is large, visible, usually loosely organized, and easy to penetrate, while R is small, "invisible" (by training and doctrine),[1] tightly organized, highly security-conscious, and hard to penetrate. Hence, this chapter will be more concerned with the operations of A than with those of R.

Information Costs and Availabilities

As discussed earlier, many current views of insurgent conflicts—the ones we have called "hearts-and-minds" views—stress those characteristics of the less developed countries (LDCs) that influence the *demand* for rebellion.[2] At the same time, these views often neglect the characteristics of the LDC environment that influence the *supply* of rebellion: that make it easier for R to get started, and harder for A to detect until it has reached a stage of organizational firmness where the chance of aborting it is lost, and the costs of controlling it have risen.

Perhaps the most significant characteristic of the LDCs, in this connection, is the high cost of information. In the LDCs, the

[1] See Chapter 4, pp. 63-68.
[2] See Chapters 2 and 3.

cost of "finding out" is usually high (almost regardless of what it is that is being investigated); the time required to obtain information is long; and the reliability of what is obtained is low. Analyzing "opportunities for organization" of the Chinese Communist Party's armed forces in the late thirties, Mao observes:

> When we are devoting ourselves to warfare in an open region, it is the . . . areas with a low cultural level, where communications are difficult and facilities for transmitting correspondence are inadequate, that are advantageous. [3]

Less developed countries are usually "plural" economies and societies, as we have noted earlier.[4] Linkages among the component parts are much less reticulated than in the more developed countries (MDCs). Flows of information, as well as of commodities and people, across the component units are relatively limited, and reliable and timely information about activities in the disparate units is scarce and expensive. From the standpoint of facilitating R, the infrequency and unreliability of contact and communication are no less important, but are usually given much less emphasis than popular grievances and discontents.

The contrast afforded by the quality, timeliness, and availability of information in the MDCs is striking. Information is abundantly available: information concerning people, products, prices, traffic flows, purchases and sales, borrowing and lending, payments and receipts, and so on and on. Easy and rapid checks can be made of residence, credit standing, schooling, family background, fingerprints, and, with slightly more difficulty, employment, occupation, and income. The freedom of choice available to people in the more developed noncommunist countries is enhanced by an abundance of accessible information on the possible choices, as well as on the options chosen. And the wide assortment of channels for tracing people and activities, through private as well as government sources,

---

[3] Mao, **Basic Tactics**, p. 69.
[4] See Chapter 3, pp. 30-32.

provides information that increases the effectiveness of preventing, as well as punishing, violation of the law. [5]

This easy access to extensive, timely, and reliable information in the MDCs means that A is likely to have warning of potential threats against it. This is particularly true where the potential threats are accompanied by organization and by political purposiveness, which implies prior planning and hence greater exposure to tracing. Violence, indeed even quite large-scale violence, can still occur in the MDCs. Events in various American cities, as well as in Paris and Rome, in recent years make this point clear. Nevertheless, while the magnitude of such violence can be large, its quality is likely to differ from that which constitutes the grit of rebellion. Violence in the MDC environment is more likely to be of the "hot" kind that erupts quickly, without the organization, planning, and purposiveness that the "cool" violence of R requires. Cool violence involves

---

[5] The following incident provides a suggestive example of how the private sector participates actively in linking information collection and dissemination with law enforcement by public authorities. When one of the authors made a purchase at a local store, he observed that the charging of the purchase to his account was accompanied by a call from the salesman to the store's credit bureau. In response to his question as to what the call was intended to accomplish, the salesman said it provided an opportunity to check whether the credit card had been stolen. The salesman related an incident that had occurred a few weeks before when a man came in and made a credit purchase. The salesman called the credit bureau, which advised him that the credit card had been stolen during a burglary several weeks earlier. He delayed the customer a few minutes; the store detective appeared and arrested him.

In this case, a private for-profit corporation finds it to its own advantage to maintain a service which collates information from various sources, including the police, and operates as a complement to established law-enforcement agencies. This kind of function and service is nonexistent in most LDCs. The usual measures of the cost of information (in terms of message units, or telephone or teletype service) within the LDCs drastically underestimate the extent to which the real costs of obtaining, storing, and using information exceed those prevailing in the MDCs. This is because a considerable part of the **social** costs of obtaining information in the MDCs is diffused throughout the society, and is borne by **private** institutions, as in the incident just described, as well as by public agencies. As a result, the costs of obtaining information in particular cases and for particular purposes are substantially reduced.

In considering information and intelligence in the LDCs, local law-enforcement agencies can perhaps make better use than they normally do of the services of private economic organizations—whose main aim is **not** law enforcement—to improve the collection and utilization of information that would assist in strengthening law and order.

premeditation and calculation, which increase the risk of detection and prevention in the MDC environment. [6]

Some exceptions to these points must be made for the university campuses of MDCs. As the experience of the late nineteen sixties in the United States and most other MDCs has shown, campus authorities sometimes were ill-informed about preparatory efforts that were underway to disrupt them. More often, and increasingly, A's information improved, but it remained exceedingly reluctant to react with preventive severity against the student rebels under the circumstances and for the reasons described earlier. [7]

In the plural environment of the LDCs, where information is expensive, unreliable, and usually delayed, cool violence is more feasible. R can organize and move from preparation to direct action (from a "preconditions" stage to a "take-off" stage, to use the earlier analogy from the economic growth literature) with relatively little advance warning, awareness, and preparation by A. Thus, the supply of R is facilitated by the inaccessibility (or high costs) of reliable and timely information. By the same token, effective counterrebellion requires that A improve its capacity to collect, store, collate, evaluate, retrieve, and use information. That is, A must seek to surmount the barriers that the LDC environment normally presents to improved performance in these activities. Contrary to the hearts-and-minds view, improved information-handling probably has a higher value for A than conferring benefits or widening suffrage; while for R, interdicting the flow of accurate and timely information to A is as important as, in the LDC environment, it is feasible.

Each of the four tasks into which we have previously divided counterinsurgency [8] depends critically on information. To restrict R's access to inputs, A must know where the inputs come from, how they are distributed, how transactions are consummated, and what the nodes or choke points in the distribution system are. Impeding the conversion of inputs into R's activities

[6] This is not to say that "cool" violence cannot occur (it does), only that it is less likely; nor that A, in MDCs, cannot be disrupted by hot violence. It can be. However, the quantity of violence that is needed is probably greater where the violence is hot than where it is cool, and certainly is greater in the MDCs where the authority structure is firmer

[7] See Chapter 6, pp. 115-117.

[8] See Chapter 5.

and forces depends on actions by A which require much improved intelligence about R: infiltrating R's own organization, spreading misinformation within it, attracting wavering (and preferably leading) figures away from it and the like.[9] Conducting counterforce operations against R is also more sensitive to reliable and timely intelligence than in other conflict situations because, as noted earlier, R's forces eschew a territorial base and are more mobile, dispersed, and immersed in the population.

Finally, strengthening A's capacity to absorb R's pressure, while A grows stronger or at least grows no weaker, is likely to depend on how well A can improve its ability to handle and use intelligence information. In trying to "harden" rural hamlets and build up local defensive militia with the proper training and equipment, A can do better if it has more information on such subjects as how R operates, when it is likely to attack, in units of what size, and, above all, whether A can adapt its own behavior to variations in these tactics. Moreover, in eliciting behavior from the population which will increase the manning and improve the performance of local defensive paramilitary forces, A needs an active counterintelligence effort to meet R's anticipated efforts to infiltrate and disrupt these forces.

Perhaps more valuable to A than any of these kinds of information about R is A's possession of a capability to discriminate between those who cooperate with A and those who do not, and to apply this knowledge accurately in its targeting. Information-handling is crucial for such discrimination. To be effective, however, the information must be closely coupled with technologies for delivering penalties that minimize error. When the Berkeley police in May 1969 employed tear gas sprayed (in a strong breeze!) from a helicopter, and fired buckshot to disperse student militants, they struck the innocent (killing one of them) as well as the offenders. Weaponry, not information, was the source of targeting error, and its effect was to weaken A's position and strengthen support for the student rebels. Similarly, when the police moved to clear a university building that militant students had occupied at Harvard in April 1969, lack of precision in targeting and delivery damaged the respect accorded the Administration, and temporarily radicalized much of the

[9] See this chapter, pp. 142-144.

student body. Compared with approximately 140 occupants of the building who were arrested, 20 bystanders outside were injured by the police, 10 non-occupants were arrested by mistake, and about 70 occupants got away!

There is perhaps nothing more likely to enhance A's legitimacy and respect than a demonstrated capacity to locate its proper target accurately, and to make the punishment (as well as the reward) fit the crime, both in severity and timeliness.[10] On the other hand, "legitimacy" is likely to be short-lived if it lacks such a capacity to discriminate. To increase A's capacity to absorb R's output requires that A demonstrate a capacity for selective and discriminating action, and this depends heavily on A's ability to collect and profit from information about the behavior of the population. The same holds for R, but usually (as noted above) the acquisition of such a capability is less difficult for it—and often R is more aware than A of the value of such efforts.

Trade-Offs Among Information, Firepower, and Mobility

Information, then, is more important in insurgent and counterinsurgent conflicts than in other forms of conflict. If, for example, one defines a side's capabilities in terms of intelligence information (measured as the probability of observing or locating some activity or target), firepower (tons of ordnance deliverable per unit of time), and mobility (cargo or personnel lift capability per unit of time), improvements in intelligence are likely to be more important (productive) than increases in mobility or firepower.[11]

The reasons for the relatively greater importance of intelligence follow from the previous discussion of the four component tasks of counterinsurgency. Controlling R's inputs, interdicting R's conversion mechanism, and strengthening A's absorptive

---

[10] See the extensive discussion of coercion and countercoercion, and the role of discrimination in such efforts, Chapter 6.

[11] Given certain assumptions about the costs of obtaining such improvements in intelligence compared with the costs of incremental firepower and mobility, it follows that incremental resources devoted to improvement in intelligence would be more efficiently used than elsewhere.

capacity all acquire enhanced importance in counterinsurgency, as compared with other forms of conflict; and intelligence information is, in turn, of relatively greater importance in these tasks than is firepower or mobility. Even the counterforce component depends more on detailed information, in counterinsurgency, than on the other ingredients, because of the nonterritorial characteristic of R's forces. The adversary's forces are more mobile and harder to locate than in other forms of conflict, so detailed information about them will be needed. With good information, modest firepower can be very effective in counterforce operations against R; without it, firepower will be wasted or even harmful to A, due to mistargeting.

Moreover, in counterinsurgency, the relatively greater importance of R's leadership, compared with its rank and file, means that capturing or killing a key leader is worth many units of R's forces. And this form of micro-targeting is highly dependent on intelligence. Recall the earlier reference to Magsaysay's strategy of "targeting" R's leadership, and his singular success in acquiring a large proportion of the Huks' top leadership in a Manila raid in 1954, as a result of good information. Desmond Palmer makes the same point about Malaya:

> Successful elimination of one well-known leader whose name conjures up terror to the inhabitants of an area, may well be more effective than the elimination of two-thirds of a guerrilla squad. [12]

If information is more important to A when fighting R than in other types of conflict, its usefulness to A also varies inversely with the level attained by R: the earlier the stage of R, the greater the chance that timely information will enable A to make it fail. As R moves toward higher levels, the conflict begins to resemble a conventional one, and the trade-offs alluded to become more similar to those in conventional conflicts. While intelligence is relatively more important in all stages of counterinsurgency than in other types of conflict, its primacy—in relationship to firepower and mobility—is more pronounced, the earlier the stage of R. These points on the several comparisons we have been discussing (between intelligence and other ingredi-

---

[12] Desmond Palmer, **The Counterintelligence Organization in an Insurgency,** unpublished paper, July, 1966, p. 26.

ents of conflict, and between insurgent conflicts and other forms of conflict) can be made more precise with the aid of a simple descriptive model, as set forth in the Appendix to this chapter.

Possibly, too, the indirect payoffs from improved intelligence are also higher in counterinsurgency than in other conflicts. Accordingly, intelligence may provide a means by which an escalating process of increased effectiveness is apt to result from an initial improvement of A's intelligence capability. Positive feedbacks are numerous and strong in the chain that connects intelligence to progress in counterinsurgency. As Thompson puts it:

> Good intelligence leads to more frequent . . . contacts. More contacts lead to more kills. These in turn lead to greater confidence in the population, resulting in better intelligence and still more contacts and kills. [13]

Imbedded in this positive feedback chain, and probably largely accounting for it, is the response of the population to a changing environment. As improved intelligence makes the conflict go more favorably for a certain side, giving information to that side appears less dangerous because its capacity for providing protection against reprisals from the other side rises. Furthermore, contributing information may itself be sensed as an effective act rather than a vain gesture: intelligence and assistance is provided to the side which now appears more likely to win (and is then also more likely viewed as deserving to do so).

Yet, this tendency, of course, may be offset by a countervailing penchant to "let George do it," particularly to the extent that the other side—though losing—increases penalties on the population's hostile behavior. Indeed, a losing side may even overcompensate by shifting its declining resources more toward such "micro-damage" activities intended to control the population, and away from guerrilla combat.

Techniques and Operations

Hearts-and-minds views of counterinsurgency often recognize the importance of information, but they view the process by

[13] Thompson, **op. cit.**, p. 89.

which it is acquired as simple if popular support is on one's side, and impossible, as well as repugnant, if the population is either hostile or *attentiste*. The notion that intelligence is a complex technical problem that can be handled efficiently or inefficiently, responsibly or irresponsibly, and that these differences require careful study and analysis is usually odious to those holding these views.

One effect of these attitudes is that when the United States gets involved in counterinsurgency conflicts, intelligence planning and operations do not receive the allocation of attention, brains, and resources their importance warrants. These attitudes and the priorities they generate need to be reversed. The analysis and understanding of intelligence should be made as respectable as its central importance in counterinsurgency requires. Thompson reflects this orientation:

> If subversion is the main threat, starting as it does well before an open insurgency and continuing through it and even afterwards, it follows that within the government the intelligence organization is of paramount importance. In fact, I would go so far as to say that no government can hope to defeat a communist insurgent movement unless it gives top priority to, and is successful in, building up such an organization.[14]

The ingredients of effective intelligence organization and operations are numerous and complex. An effective system requires not just collection of information from multiple sources (some degree of redundancy is essential) but also processing, classifying, evaluating, storing, and retrieving information. Indeed, modern technological progress in information processing and handling is probably more important for counterinsurgency than are changes in weapons technology.

As a part of intelligence operations, A must be able to communicate information to the population and the rebels. When the population is the audience, the aim of communicating is to identify the kind of behavior that is sought and the kind of behavior that is discouraged, with clear indication of the consequences attached to each behavior: the carrot and the stick, each adequately publicized. When R is the audience, A needs to communicate in-

---

[14] Thompson, **op. cit.,** p. 84.

formation relating to the structure of rewards for defection, the speed and reliability with which such rewards will be paid, and the protection that will accompany payment.

Once having communicated to the population, A must be in a position to observe their behavior, distinguish compliant from noncompliant behavior, and control resources for applying rewards or punishments, accordingly. The demands thereby placed on the intelligence system require that it be closely linked to the command and control of A's entire operations. For this reason, as well as others, A's intelligence operations must be strong and unified. The role of the Special Branch in the British command structure in Malaya is a model: standing astride all intelligence and counterintelligence activities (both police and military), and with its direction tightly linked with the top-command structure under Sir Gerald Templar.[15] This central and crucial role contrasts rather strikingly with the overlapping, muzzy organizational separation of intelligence and command functions in operations against the Viet Cong in Vietnam.[16]

In conducting intelligence operations, A must be able to acquire information *about* R, as well as cause misinformation *within* R. A's ability to increase its information about R depends fundamentally on being able to provide security and protection to the population, or at least to selected components of the population, in combination with rewards and penalties. What is not usually recognized, however, is that the provision of protection and security is not an all-or-nothing affair, that it can be done in various ways, and that the various ways depend as much (or more) on dexterity and ingenuity as on force.

One means of providing protection is by preserving anonymity. An example is the familiar device of the "little booth" into which everybody in a village is compelled to pass. The point is to coerce everyone into the role of *possible* informer; the informer is rendered untargetable because he is anonymously immersed in a sea of non-informers. Universality confers anonymity, and anonymity confers security. Thus in Malaya

[15] See Thompson, **op. cit.,** pp. 81-83, 85; and Clutterbuck, **op. cit.,** pp. 56-59, 100. The Head of Special Branch was the No. 3 man in the entire command structure in the Malayan counterinsurgency operation.

[16] Desmond Palmer also stresses the importance of centralized intelligence operations in counterinsurgency. For example, "To be able to act with the speed required means that all collateral intelligence must be available in one place and ready for quick use." Palmer, **op. cit.,** p. 29.

. . . the police would surround a village during curfew and leave a piece of blank paper at every house; in the morning they would let [require?] each villager [to] drop his paper [unmarked except for the information itself] into a . . . box, which was later opened at police headquarters, with the anonymity of the informants thus . . . protected.[17]

In another variant, A arrests a large number of people, among whom the informer (already known to A) finds himself, and then releases them all together.

Informers may be protected by rendering them unidentifiable to the adversary in other ways. Thus in Kenya

. . . [through] the use of hooded men. These were captured Mau-Mau willing to . . . identify their former associates. . . . A dozen or more of them were . . . seated in a line of canvas booths and suspects were slowly led past them. If a hooded man recognized a suspect as a member of Mau-Mau, he merely held up his hand and when the escorting officer walked across to him he gave him the details in a whisper. . . . Men frequently broke out in a sweat or trembled uncontrollably as they faced the line of informers . . . many of them broke down.[18]

An alternative means for providing protection is simply to render an informer inaccessible to R by evacuating the informer and his family to a geographically remote area, or to a fortified settlement.[19]

Either side obviously can benefit from causing misinformation to circulate within the opponent's organization—for example, by arousing false suspicions about the reliability of its members. Valeriano recounts how the location of a Huk unit in the Philippines was sometimes accompanied by a simple ruse: an L-5 plane would fly over the unit, and, though under fire, the pilot,

---

[17] Statement by Captain Anthony S. Jeapes, R-412-ARPA, p. 108.

[18] Majdalany, **op. cit.**, p. 208.

[19] The French made use of this technique in Algeria, combined with heavy emphasis on punishment for noninformers. It is hard to see how the French practice of evacuating informers from their native villages to the city of Algiers could have elicited confidence on the part of a would-be informer that he would be inaccessible to the Liberation Front! Patrick Kessel and Giovanni Pirelli, **Le Peuple Algerien et La Guerre** (Paris: Francois Maspers, 1962), p. 386, Our translation.

using an electric megaphone, would say (to the supposed informer) as a parting sally:

> Thank you very much, friend down below. By your information we have been able to contact your friends. Be very careful, I hope you have not exposed yourself unnecessarily! [20]

Edward Lansdale has observed that this tactic

> . . . frequently caused as many casualties to the enemy as a fire fight. As the enemy withdrew, he would hold kangaroo courts. [21]

Compromising members of R by acknowledging (falsely) their help can also be used to reach R's civil infrastructure. Valeriano, for example, recounts how he was able to dislodge a village mayor whom he knew to be a Huk sympathizer, but who had political influence in Manila which made his removal difficult. After an accidental and successful encounter outside the village, some of the Huk dead were brought into the village:

> When a large crowd had assembled and the mayor was about to inspect the bodies, Colonel Valeriano stepped up and loudly thanked him 'for the information that led to the killing of these two men.' . . . the mayor fled to Manila the next day [22]

Another technique for causing misinformation within the opponent's organization is, of course, the use of infiltrators whose task may be eased by causing false confidence within the other side which enables its guard to be penetrated. Where R's communications are primitive, as is usually the case, any operation that results in scattering the guerrillas affords A an increased opportunity for infiltrating them. Their lack of good local communication systems puts them:

---

[20] Valeriano, RM-3652-PR, .pp. 49-50. The ruse was accompanied by calling out the names of the Huk leaders in the unit that had been located, using individual names drawn from the government's own intelligence files, though imputed to the "friend down below."

[21] **Ibid.**, p. 50.

[22] R-412-ARPA, p. 76.

. . . at a loss to tell the difference between an unknown guerrilla unit that is genuine and one that is a plant. [23]

Infiltration can be facilitated by fabricating a highly plausible record for the penetrators. One means of doing so is by according them the same severe treatment that the opponent's genuine members receive. For example, in the Philippines

Colonel Valeriano . . . staged sham battles in front of local villages between uniformed forces and some of his men dressed in Huk clothes. After tying them up and manhandling them a little, the soldiers would turn the pseudo-Huks over to the police for safekeeping . . . when they finally came out of prison, the men had a great deal of information. . . . [24]

Once a side becomes aware that infiltration has occurred, the false suspicion and unjust punishments that may be provoked may have a more deleterious effect than the infiltration itself: that is, the second-order impact of the infiltrators may be greater than the first-order impact. [25]

In collecting accurate information, as distinct from causing the circulation of misinformation, what we have discussed earlier is in the realm of "micro" tactics and operations: mainly those concerned with specific tricks, devices, stratagems. At the broader, "macro" level, probably the main requisite is to set up a structured and protected *market* for the kind of information that A wants. While sources of information need tight protection—through anonymity, as well as direct protection, as described earlier—the structure of the market itself (that is, the prices to be paid for different types of information, a system for quickly cross-checking new information against previously available data, quick and reliable payments, and the like) needs to be highly publicized and reliably implemented. The returns from this form of endeavor can be extremely high to A. From some empirical work on Malaya, it appears that the returns (in terms of communist guerrillas "acquired" by capture, surrender, or elimination) per dollar expended on information exceeded by more than

[23] Galula, R-412-ARPA, p. 47.

[24] R-412-ARPA, p. 48.

[25] For an illustration of this pattern, see the American reaction to the infiltration of Otto Skorzeny's Special Troops among separated American units in the Ardennes in 1944: **Readings in Guerrilla Warfare,** U.S. Army Special Warfare School, Fort Bragg, N.C., December, 1960, pp. 29-30.

tenfold the returns per dollar expended on firepower in the Malayan emergency. [26]

The more one shifts emphasis from the demand side of R to its supply, to the factors influencing the ease or difficulty of R's start and growth, the more important does intelligence become. In the conduct of an effective counterrebellion, intelligence operations demand the highest priority in resources, people, and ingenuity. Indeed, for counterrebellion to be waged at budget levels that make the prospects look more encouraging to A (including its external sources of support) than to potential Rs (including their external sources of support), the relative allocation of scarce resources to intelligence is likely to be high.

It should be evident that the problem of intelligence and information in the "third world"—the LDCs—is exceedingly complex, and deeply imbedded in the characteristics of these societies. The difficulty (or, put another way, the high cost) of obtaining reliable information is highly correlated with many other structural characteristics of these societies. But the fact that cost of information is correlated (negatively) with per capita income, urbanization, longevity, literacy, industrialization, political participation, and the like does not necessarily mean that improving information flows must be merged with these other major problems. To some extent, the information and intelligence problem can be approached, and solutions found, *separately* from many of the other problems of modernization in the third world. Improved intelligence, like improved counterinsurgency more generally, is related to but by no means identical with the solution of the basic structural problems of development. To say that the latter must be solved before the former is to establish goals that are unreasonably and unrealistically ambitious.

It may be worthwhile to conclude with some cautionary observations about the impact of programs directed specifically toward improving information acquisition and dissemination in the third world. Improved informational capabilities are likely to be crucial, if vulnerability to and incidence of insurgency are to be reduced. At the same time, improvements in these capabilities provide instruments with which more efficiently repressive

---

[26] Cf. RM-3651-PR; G. J. Pauker, **Notes on Nonmilitary Measures in Control of Insurgency,** The RAND Corporation, P-2642, October, 1962, Santa Monica, California; H. Speier, **Revolutionary War,** P-3445, September, 1966. Other work on the Philippines, although based on even less complete data, suggests similar results.

dictatorships can be developed. This is another example of the general proposition that programs and techniques that may be supported in the underdeveloped countries with *one* set of intended objectives (for example, deterring or meeting communist insurgencies), may turn out to be used for quite *different* purposes in practice. Precautions can and should be taken, and some degree of control and leverage can be maintained to reduce the risk of misuse, particularly where U.S. support is involved. But a fundamental dilemma remains: reducing the risk of effective insurgency may—under certain circumstances—increase the risk of oppressive abuse of the capabilities created with this aim in mind. Efforts to solve one problem may lead to other, perhaps worse problems—a danger to be kept well in mind. Forewarning is, to some extent, forearming—but *only* to some extent.

Appendix to Chapter 7

Trade-offs Among Information, Firepower, and Mobility: A Simple Descriptive Model

The following simple model expresses the point of view advanced in this chapter concerning trade-offs among information, firepower, and mobility, according to various levels of conflict or various stages of insurgency.

Let

E_i = military effectiveness in various conflicts (the i's can be thought of either as different stages of insurgency, or as different levels of violence rising from insurgency to conventional conflicts, $i = 1, 2, \ldots, n$)

I_i = information (in terms of the probability of observing or locating some activity or target)

F_i = firepower (in tons of ordnance deliverable per hour)

M_i = mobility (in terms of cargo or personnel lift capabilities per hour)

Then, in relation to the discussion in Chapter VII,

$$E_i = \alpha \, I_i{}^{\alpha_i} \; F_i{}^{\beta_6}, \; M_i{}^{\gamma_i} \tag{1}$$

Thus,

$$\alpha = f(i), \; \beta = g(i), \; \gamma = h(i) \tag{2}$$

If one accepts this discussion, for an early stage of R ($i=1$),

$$\alpha > \gamma > \beta \tag{2a}$$

for a later stage ($i=2$),

$$\gamma > \alpha > \beta \tag{2b}$$

and for a still later stage ($i=3$),

$$\beta > \gamma > \alpha \tag{2c}$$

Differentiating the effectiveness function partially with respect to I, F, and M, in succession, and dividing the partial derivatives, the marginal rates of substitution among information, firepower, and mobility are:

$$\frac{d\ I}{d\ F} = -\frac{\beta_i}{\alpha_i}\frac{I}{F} \tag{3}$$

$$\frac{d\ I}{d\ M} = -\frac{\gamma_i}{\alpha_i}\frac{I}{M} \tag{4}$$

$$\frac{d\ M}{d\ F} = -\frac{\beta_i}{\gamma_i}\frac{M}{F} \tag{5}$$

Thus, the relative importance of information with respect to firepower (mobility) would be greater, the lower the stage of insurgency being considered, and the less information available to the authorities to start with.

Chapter 8

REBELLION AND AUTHORITY:
A SUMMARY

The primary aim of this book is generalization and theory: to advance hypotheses and illustrate them by referring to specific cases. In concluding we shall try to summarize the main hypotheses and issues for further study, as they have emerged in the preceding chapters.

The Principal Theme

Perhaps the most general point that recurs in the book is this: for R to win, it *need not* initially have the spontaneous support, sympathy, or loyalty of the people, not even of a significant minority of the people, although it may in fact enjoy such support. Moreover, even fairly far along in the struggle, R can make substantial progress *without* substantial popular endorsement, though it may have acquired it in a significant number of cases. Thorough organization and effective coercion can enjoin or engender particular modes of behavior by the population, notwithstanding popular preferences that would lead to different behavior if a purely voluntary choice could be made.[1] The trade-off involved here is an unpleasant reality. By the same

[1] In the words of one former Viet Cong combat leader who was interviewed by RAND personnel after he rallied to the GVN in 1967: "We knew the people wanted nothing but peace for themselves . . . we had no illusion that they were for us . . . we knew that when we left they'd serve the GVN . . . the people would submit to whoever was wearing a gun."

token, if an A quells an R, this does not signify that the A has—
or deserves—genuine support from the people. Evil governments
may quell virtuous rebellions, and virtuous governments may
lose to evil rebellions. While Leo Durocher's pronouncement that
"good guys finish last" is not necessarily correct, neither is it
correct to assume that a "good" side (whether A or R) will win
over a "bad" side. Obviously, this does not simplify the choice
facing U.S. policy of whether to support, oppose, or ignore a
particular A or R. Successful insurgencies are not necessarily
detrimental to U.S. interests, nor are successful counterinsurgencies necessarily advantageous.

Hearts-and-Minds Versus Systems

A widely held theory about R contends that popular attitudes, sympathy, and support play the decisive role in enabling
rebellion to get started, gain momentum, and win. This view,
which we have characterized as the hearts-and-minds theory, influences and perhaps dominates much discussion and thinking
about this range of problems. The main characteristics of this
theory contrast sharply with those of an alternative approach advanced in this study. The main characteristics of the prevailing
view are:
1. Emphasis on popular support based on ardor and preferences.
2. Stress on internal grievances and other internal influences
(endogeny), and a discounting of the effects of external influence
and support (exogeny), in the genesis of rebellion.
3. Emphasis on economic deprivation and inequality as
influences on the strength of an emerging R.
4. A conception of insurgent conflict in terms of electoral
analogies, according to which the progress of each side is influenced by and reflects the prevailing affiliations of a majority,
or a substantial minority, of the people.
The alternative approach advanced here differs on each of
these points, and involves a different framework for analyzing
the problem.
1. The alternative approach suggests that population behavior depends not only on likes and dislikes, but also on the
opportunities and costs confronting the populace in choosing

whether and to what extent to indulge their preferences. (And the choice itself will, in its turn, affect preferences.) In other words, the progress and process of R depend not only on "demand" conditions—that is, on preferences—but also on "supply" conditions, which relate to the cost and effectiveness of the R organization itself.

2. As influences on these supply conditions, internal factors are important. Perhaps some minimum threshold of internal demand conditions is necessary for the supply process to get going at all. But this minimum is likely to exist throughout the less developed world, and elsewhere too, for some considerable time. Above the minimum, a wide range of external factors also matter, and indeed "trade off" against the internal factors. Given some minimal level of the internal environment, external resources and skill can substitute for internal factors in producing and sustaining an R.

3. Within considerable ranges and over considerable time, economic development and improved distribution of its fruits, while strongly desirable goals in themselves, may be as likely to facilitate as to hinder the process by which an astute R grows. The actual outcome will depend on the balance among the income effects, substitution effects, and preference effects of development; and a presumption that this outcome will usually help the A is *not* warranted.

4. Finally, the alternative approach suggests that the progress made by each side in the conflict influences the affiliations of most of the population as much as, or more than, it is influenced *by* those affiliations.

Analytically, our view of insurgency divides the problem into several parts corresponding to the components of the insurgent system: the *sources of inputs* (people, food, materiel, information), and the terms (costs) on which inputs are obtainable from internal and external sources; the mechanism for *converting* the inputs (through indoctrination, training, logistic support, and operations) into activities or outputs; and the *targeting* of these activities against the existing social and political structure. Operationally, the problem of counterinsurgency can be divided into several tasks relating to these components of the system: (a) the counterproduction task of impeding the availability of inputs and the efficiency with which they are converted by the R organization into outputs; (b) the counterforce task, involving the destruction of outputs or forces produced by the R system; and (c) the task of building the structure of A so that it can absorb and outlast the insurgent competition.

The Rebellion's Viewpoint and Characteristics

How does an R fit into this framework? What are its propensities and how does it operate? In general, the task of an emerging R is to join the demand for its services—based on existing frictions and discontent—with the efficient supply of these services, where efficiency entails both capitalizing on existing demands and building and intensifying them. In the course of its growth, the insurgent management makes successive choices of targets for its activities. Should it eliminate the resented and low-performing officials of the existing regime, or the better and more respected ones? Targeting the low performers enhances the probability of endorsement by the population, thereby minimizing the risk of counteraction and informing. Targeting the high performers may evoke acceptance from the population because of the respect and fear which such a message of apparent invincibility conveys. While both patterns are exemplified in the varied historical experience of insurgent conflicts, the hypothesis emerges that as a rebellion grows in strength it is likely to move from targeting the "bad" low-performers to targeting the "good" high-performers.

Various attributes of R characterize its doctrine and operations, and sharply distinguish it from a typical A. For example, it is characteristic of R to preach and practice austerity in individual behavior, and economy of effort in organizational activity. R tends to be dedicated to efficiency and austerity—in other words, to a cost-effectiveness calculus which distinguishes it from the propensities of conventional As and their military establishments. Learning, adaptability, and flexibility tend to be cardinal virtues in R's doctrine.

In its operational doctrine, R emphasizes staying power rather than firepower, endurance and attrition rather than traditional victory. Indeed, resisting the temptation to grasp at victory by "going conventional" is emphasized and lauded. Instead of early victory, R extols stealth, evasion, planned retreat, and nonattachment to territory. High performance for R thus consists precisely of those tactical attributes that conventional military doctrine regards as demeaning: retreat, evasion, escape, hiding, evacuation of territory (and conscious disinterest in the forward edge of the battle area, or FEBA, so beloved by conventional military theorists), austerity, and stamina.

There is an intimate connection between these tenets of R's doctrine, and the structural characteristics of the less developed countries for which the doctrine has been articulated. To be mobile, flexible, unattached to territory, enamored of retreat, and prideful of staying power, R must retain a low degree of visibility when it chooses to. It can be hypothesized that the visibility of insurgent organization and operation varies inversely with the level of economic development. Hence, underdeveloped countries provide congenial conditions for propitiating R, although Rs may arise in advanced countries too.

The Authority's Viewpoint and Characteristics

How does the problem look to A? What are the concepts and tactics of A for deterring or meeting the threat of rebellion? How does this threat compare with other threats—for example, the conventional threat of external aggression—facing A?

The standard view is that A's problem in deterring or meeting an R is basically a political, rather than a military, one. In this view, the threat of an R and the design of solutions to meet it are held to differ fundamentally from other threats to which A is exposed. For example, the threat of external aggression is usually viewed as principally a military rather than a political problem. The approach advanced in Chapter 5 diverges from this standard approach.

While accepting the difference between insurgent conflicts and other conflicts, our view is that the difference is not accurately or adequately expressed in terms of the usual contrast between the primacy of politics and that of force. Rather, the contrast between Rs and other threats lies *within* these categories, not *between* them. The kinds of force and the types of political performance that an A must sustain to deter or meet insurgent conflicts differ from those required to meet other threats.

For example, if A is to apply force effectively in insurgent conflicts, it must have capabilities much closer to R's than to the capabilities of conventional forces. Mobility, reconnaissance, police (rather than military) intelligence, a capacity for operating effectively in small units, and police and paramilitary forces are the important military elements for deterring or meeting the threat of R—*not* armor, artillery, jet aircraft, and large centralized operations by large divisional units.

Politically, the capabilities that A must develop and demonstrate involve the capacity to act with speed, consistency, and discrimination. More specifically, A must protect the population; identify desired behavior and reward it by effective programs; and withhold such programs in areas that have failed to perform in desirable ways. A must demonstrate a capacity to act with discrimination and restraint, basing its action on legal and orderly processes that provide a contrast to the putative illegality and disorder of R.

A's tactics for employing force effectively also differ appreciably from effective tactics in other wars. By contrast with conventional conflicts, in which counterforce and pro-territory objectives are primary, the aim of successful tactics in insurgent conflicts is counterproduction: to impair the ability of the R to produce and reproduce forces, while "hardening" the structure of government authority so that it can withstand R's attacks and permit the essential counterproduction effort to gain momentum. The organization of R, and its interface with the population, is the crucial target for A's military and political efforts—not R's forces themselves, or the transient territorial base from which R operates.

Under these circumstances, the task of measuring A's success is different from and more difficult than measuring success in other conflicts. Counterforce and pro-territory indicators are not of primary relevance. Instead, to be really confident of the effectiveness of A's efforts requires a detailed knowledge of how R's own organization is faring: its cohesiveness or fragmentation; the terms on which it is obtaining inputs from internal or external sources; the efficiency with which the inputs are being converted into forces and activities; and the reputation that A itself is acquiring among the population for effectiveness, discrimination, and merit.

To know all this places heavy demands on A's intelligence

system, not only in waging effective counterinsurgency, but in evaluating how the effort is proceeding and feeding back the results of this evaluation into the adjustment and improvement of the effort itself.

If there is a single, relatively reliable indicator of A's success in controlling an ongoing R, it is the rate at which middle- and higher-level officers and cadres in R's organization are "acquired" by A, whether by defection or by capture. Because R's regeneration coefficient (the ratio of reproducible rank and file to cadre) is apt to be high, as long as its organization core remains intact, so do its strength and stamina. Depleting the core of the organization—acquiring the cadres—should therefore be A's aim. In successful counterinsurgencies, such as in Malaya and the Philippines, this indicator has usually been a good predictor of progress. And it has never been deceptively high in counterinsurgencies that have been unsuccessful, probably also because it is harder to falsify than the more familiar counter-force and pro-territory indicators.

Damage and Coercion from Both Sides

Unfortunately, the contest between R and A is often as much a contest in the effective management of coercion as a contest for the hearts and minds of the people. So it becomes relevant to examine the contrasting styles of R and A in threatening and inflicting damage, and to seek to understand the content of successful and unsuccessful coercion in insurgent conflict.

In general, there is a sharp contrast between R and A with respect to the style and effectiveness with which they use the threat and the imposition of damage. The pattern employed by R is usually strikingly more effective. Whereas R's doctrine acknowledges a central role for coercion and would optimize the use of this instrument, A's doctrine—especially that of As professing a democratic ideological stance—abjures damage-infliction against the population as a declaratory stance. (The stance obviously contrasts with the typical A's stress on counterforce, damage-inflicting tactics in dealing with the organized military forces of the adversary.) In the case of A, damage-infliction on the population usually emerges as fallout from other activities rather than as conscious design. As a result, the quantum of damage inflicted by A is often inflated and capricious rather than limited and discriminating. The latter attributes would only be likely to follow explicit acknowledgment of the role of coercion—an acknowledgment A's public stance usually makes it unwilling to accept.

Thus, "hot" violence—that is, damage without calculation and from motives of frustration, hate, or cruelty—tends to be more characteristic of A than R; while "cool" violence tends to characterize the operations of the rebellion. The paradox, of course, is that the total damage inflicted by R from its vantage point of coolness may actually be substantially less than that resulting from the heat and intemperance of A. Effectiveness tends to vary inversely with temperature.

Effective coercion—"effective" in the sense of obtaining compliance from the population—depends on several specific and complex elements: (a) the degree of understanding on the part of the population as to what is intended and why; (b) the appropriateness of the penalties; (c) the extent of their enforcement through time; (d) the extent to which innocents are spared; and (e) the degree of protection available *if* compliance is forthcoming, in the face of countercoercion by the other side.

The extent and complexity of the list suggest the burden that an effective draconian stance places on the organization of either A or R in combining severity and regularity, implacability and restraint, power and predictability. It seems to be the case in less developed countries that modern R*s* are more frequently able to bear these burdens successfully than modern A*s* —perhaps because the former acknowledge the central role of coercion in conducting their activities.

While the cool analysis of coercion is morally repugnant, failure to analyze it should be even more odious, because such neglect magnifies the power of those who do analyze it. Like nuclear war, this is another case where it is necessary to think about the unthinkable.

Intelligence and Information: Needs and Dilemmas

Improved intelligence and information capabilities are central to nearly all aspects of insurgent conflict, both for R and for A. Yet achieving this improvement is most difficult in the environment of the less developed countries. In general, the costs of timely and accurate information vary inversely (and probably nonlinearly) with the level of development. Thus, it is much harder for A to obtain timely and accurate information in less developed countries than in more developed countries. In advanced countries, A's intelligence is usually much better than R's, while in the less developed countries the situation is reversed.

A corollary can be drawn from this hypothesis concerning differences between more developed countries and less developed countries with respect to the types of violence likely to be encountered there. In the former, "hot" violence—which implies spontaneity, hence a shorter preparatory period, and hence less time for possible pre-emption by A—is more likely to occur. On the other hand, in less developed countries, "cool" violence, accompanied by greater preparation and a longer lead time, is more likely; the resulting increase in the risk of being observed may be small, and the chance of being detected remains low.

While an improved capacity to obtain and make use of intelligence information is central to virtually all the tasks of counterinsurgency, its role is nowhere more crucial than in connection with the controlled use of coercion, discussed earlier. Indeed, there is probably nothing more likely to enhance the legitimacy and respect of an A in the eyes of the people than a demonstrated capacity to make the punishment (as well as the reward) fit the crime, both in severity and timeliness. Such discernment requires a capacity to ascertain who is doing what and when, with a speed and reliability seldom found among the As of the less developed countries. Consequently, improved intelligence capabilities are likely to be of great importance in insurgent conflicts, probably at least as important as the judicious distribution of benefits to the population at large.

The components of such enhanced capabilities involve: (a) collecting, processing, and retrieving information; (b) communicating clearly and regularly with the population; (c) observing behavior and responses accurately and continually; and (d) relating the foregoing components to the allocation and control of subsequent programs and action.

Although the cost of information—broadly construed—is negatively correlated with most other characteristics of economic and social development, this does not necessarily mean that the problem of improving information flows must be merged with all other development problems. To some extent, the information and intelligence problem can be approached, and solutions found, separately from other development problems. There is, of course, a profound risk in attempting to do so—namely, the risk that improvements in information and intelligence capabilities may be used to bring about or entrench repressive despots. The dilemma is a real one, not to be overlooked or dismissed lightly. On the other hand, it is in some ways only a more acute instance of a phenomenon applying generally to advanced technology and modernization in the third world—to the internal combustion engine, to the jet engine, and to nuclear explosives as well as intelligence capabilities. Programs and techniques that widen opportunities for choice may nevertheless result in undesirable consequences. Precautions can and should be taken, and some degree of control should be maintained to reduce the risk of abuse, particularly where U.S. support is involved. But the dilemma remains: reducing the risk of insurgency may carry with it the increased risk of abusing capabilities that have been created with this aim in mind.

One need not be apologetic about this dilemma, nor should one view its acceptance as "reactionary," and its denial as "progressive." Without more effective information and intelligence capabilities—indeed, without more effective capabilities for dealing with rebellion and subversion in general—authorities that are genuinely disposed toward freedom and progress can still be destroyed by oppressive rebellions. Such rebellions may then establish themselves impregnably with precisely those capabilities whose absence from the authorities' arsenal contributed to their arrival to power.

Index

Adelman, Irma, 52n
Aguinaldo, 43, 59
Algeria, 1, 14n, 40, 59, 65, 92n
    Battle of Algiers, 93, 102n
    French experience, 59, 91,
        92-94, 96, 97, 98, 100,
        102, 107, 110,
        111-112, 118, 119, 120,
        121-122, 126-127,
        128-129, 142n
    National Algerian
        Movement (MNA),
        14n
    National Liberation Front
        (FLN), 14n, 97, 100,
        102, 106
    *Organisation de l'Armée
        Secrète* (OAS), 93-94,
        96, 98
Almond, G. A., 16n
Ancien régime, reasons for
    fall, 21
Anderson, B. L., 115n
Arabs, 65, 68, 86, 93, 94, 96,
    107, 120
Asher, Robert 16n
Austerity. *See* Ideology
    (rebellion),
    puritanism
Authority:
    advantages over rebellion,
        58, 60-61, 67
    definition, 4
    legitimacy, 37, 73, 83, 137,
        154, 157

maintenance costs, 15, 57,
    62-63
    structure, 132, 135n, 152
    See also Counterrebellion

Barange, 96n
Batista regime, 14n, 72
Bell, J. Franklin, 97
Berkeley (University of
    California), 18,
    78, 130, 136
Bodard, Lucien, 13, 14n, 101n,
    106n, 107n, 109n,
    121n, 123n, 124n,
    125n, 126n, 131
Bohannan, Charles T. R., 66n,
    67n, 126n
Bonnard, Robert, 93n, 100n
Border control, 76-78
Boulding, Kenneth E., 22
Brinton, Crane, 17
Britain, 15, 62, 69, 72, 76-77,
    79, 96, 106, 113
    Royal Air Force, 72-73
Buchan, Alastair, 71n
Burma, 1, 61
Burn, A. R., 100n

Callwell, Charles E., 58, 60
Campus rebellion, v, 2, 18, 29,
    31, 54, 55, 78, 115-
    117, 129-130, 135,
    136-137
Castro, Fidel, 14n, 51, 72, 90

subordination to political
factors, 71-75, 153
technology, 61, 67, 69-70,
136, 140, 158
types of force, 71n,
72-75
Mitchell, Edward J., 21n
Modernization. *See* Less-
developed countries
(LDCs), problems of
modernization
More-developed countries
(MDCs), v, 2, 17,
29, 31, 32n, 54, 115,
133-135, 157
problems of reform, 29,
55
See also Campus
rebellion; Urban
rebellion
Morland, 96n
Morris, Cynthia Taft, 52n
Muslims, 96, 102, 112, 128,
129

Napoleon, 63, 106, 121
Nasution, Abdul Harris, 56,
63, 66, 68, 69n
National liberation wars, 6,
7, 22
Neighboring rebellions. *See*
Interdependent
rebellions
Neutrals (toward rebellion),
vii, 42, 46-47, 55,
94, 121
New York City, 12
New York Times, 6n, 19n,
40n
Nondenunciation, 10-11, 55,
102
Nuclear war, v, 22n, 51, 57,
73, 74, 75, 82, 114,156

Organization (rebellion), 2,
7, 28, 33, 48-53,
94-95
civil infrastructure, 143
compared with other
modern organiza-
tions, 48, 49, 52, 56
decisionmaking, 48
efficiency, 56-57, 94-95,
152
flexibility, 60-61, 68-69,
94-95, 152
structure, 48, 132
See also Leadership;
Personnel
Outputs (rebellion), 32, 34-40,
50n, 79-82, 137,
151-152

Palestine, 96, 113
Pallis, A. A., 59n, 62n, 69n
Palmer, Desmond, 138, 141n
Partisans. *See* World War
II, resistance in
Axis-occupied
countries
Pathet Lao, 54
Pauker, G. J., 145n
Personnel (authority):
draftees, 92-94, 121
landlords, 54-55, 116
officials, 33n, 54-55, 88,
102, 117-118, 152
police, 33n, 37, 74, 76,
78, 83, 85, 87, 118,
130, 134n, 136, 141,
142, 154
paramilitary, 37, 74, 83,
136, 154
regular military, 33n,
73, 76, 83, 85, 90-
94, 141
Personnel (rebellion), 34, 48,

Selected RAND Books

ARROW, KENNETH J. and MARVIN HOFFENBERG, *A Time Series Analysis of Interindustry Demands.* Amsterdam, Holland: North-Holland Publishing Company, July 1959.

BECKER, ABRAHAM S., *Soviet National Income 1958-1964.* Berkeley and Los Angeles: University of California Press, July 1969.

BERGSON, ABRAM, *The Real National Income of Soviet Russia Since 1928.* Cambridge, Massachusetts: Harvard University Press, November 1961.

BERGSON, ABRAM and HANS HEYMANN, JR., *Soviet National Income and Product, 1940-1948.* New York: Columbia University Press, June 1954.

BRODIE, BERNARD, *Strategy in the Missile Age.* Princeton, New Jersey: Princeton University Press, September 1959.

CHAPMAN, JANET G., *Real Wages in Soviet Russia Since 1928.* Cambridge, Massachusetts: Harvard University Press, October 1963.

DORFMAN, ROBERT, PAUL A. SAMUELSON, and ROBERT M. SOLOW, *Linear Programming and Economic Analysis.* New York: McGraw-Hill Book Company, Inc., February 1958.

DOWNS, ANTHONY, *Inside Bureaucracy.* Boston, Massachusetts: Little, Brown and Company, July 1967.

FISHMAN, GEORGE S., *Spectral Methods in Econometrics.* Cambridge, Massachusetts: Harvard University Press, July 1969.

GOLDHAMER, HERBERT and ANDREW W. MARSHALL, *Psychosis and Civilization.* Glencoe, Illinois: The Free

Press, June 1953.

HALPERN, MANFRED, *The Politics of Social Change in the Middle East and North Africa.* Princeton, New Jersey: Princeton University Press, October 1963.

HIRSHLEIFER, JACK, JAMES C. DeHAVEN, and JEROME W. MILLIMAN, *Water Supply: Economics, Technology, and Policy.* Chicago, Illinois: The University of Chicago, October 1960.

HITCH, CHARLES J. and ROLAND McKEAN, *The Economics of Defense in the Nuclear Age.* Cambridge, Massachusetts: Harvard University Press, September 1960.

HOEFFDING, OLEG, *Soviet National Income and Product in 1928.* New York: Columbia University Press, July 1954.

JOHNSON, JOHN J. (ed.), *The Role of the Military in Underdeveloped Countries.* Princeton, New Jersey: Princeton University Press, May 1962.

JOHNSON, WILLIAM A., *The Steel Industry of India.* Cambridge, Massachusetts: Harvard University Press, December 1966.

JOHNSTONE, WILLIAM C., *Burma's Foreign Policy: A Study in Neutralism.* Cambridge, Massachusetts: Harvard University Press, March 1963.

KECSKEMETI, PAUL, *The Unexpected Revolution.* Stanford, California: Stanford University Press, October 1961.

KERSHAW, JOSEPH A. and ROLAND N. McKEAN, *Teacher Shortages and Salary Schedules.* New York: McGraw-Hill Book Company, Inc., November 1962.

LEITES, NATHAN, *The Operational Code of the Politburo.* New York: McGraw-Hill Book Company, Inc., February 1951.

LEITES, NATHAN, *A Study of Bolshevism.* Glencoe, Illinois: The Free Press, December 1953.

LEITES, NATHAN and ELSA BERNAUT, *Ritual of Liquidation: The Case of the Moscow Trials.* Glencoe, Illinois: The Free Press, October 1954.

LEITES, NATHAN, *On the Game of Politics in France.* Stanford, California: Stanford University Press, April 1959.

LIU, TA-CHUNG and KUNG-CHIA YEH, *The Economy of the Chinese Mainland: National Income and Economic Development, 1933-1959.* Princeton, New Jersey: Princeton University Press, January 1965.

LUBELL, HAROLD, *Middle East Oil Crises and Western Europe's Energy Supplies*. Baltimore, Maryland: The Johns Hopkins Press, July 1963.

McKEAN, ROLAND N., *Efficiency in Government Through Systems Analysis: With Emphasis on Water Resource Development*. New York: John Wiley & Sons, Inc., June 1958.

MELNIK, CONSTANTIN and NATHAN LEITES, *The House Without Windows: France Selects a President*. Evanston, Illinois: Row, Peterson and Company, June 1958.

MOORSTEEN, RICHARD, *Prices and Production of Machinery in the Soviet Union, 1928-1959*. Cambridge, Massachusetts: Harvard University Press, June 1962.

NELSON, RICHARD R., MERTON J. PECK, and EDWARD D. KALACHEK, *Technology, Economic Growth and Public Policy*. Washington, D.C.: The Brookings Institution, January 1967.

NOVICK, DAVID (ed.), *Program Budgeting: Program Anaylsis and the Federal Budget*. Cambridge, Massachusetts: Harvard University Press, December 1965.

PINCUS, JOHN A., *Economic Aid and International Cost Sharing*. Baltimore, Maryland: The Johns Hopkins Press, August 1965.

QUADE, E. S. (ed.), *Analysis for Military Decisions*. Chicago, Illinois: Rand McNally and Company, Amsterdam, Netherlands: North Holland Publishing Company, December 1964.

QUADE, E. S., and W. I. BOUCHER, *Systems Analysis and Policy Planning: Applications in Defense*. New York, New York: American Elsevier Publishing Company, June 1968.

ROSEN, GEORGE, *Democracy and Economic Change in India*. Berkeley and Los Angeles, California: University of California Press, April 1966.

SCALAPINO, ROBERT A., *The Japanese Communist Movement*. Berkeley and Los Angeles, California: University of California Press, March 1967.

TANHAM, G. K., *Communist Revolutionary Warfare: The Vietminh in Indochina*. New York: Frederick A. Praeger, Inc., November 1961.

WHITING, ALLEN S., *China Crosses the Yalu: The Decision to Enter the Korean War*. New York: The Macmillan Company, November 1960.

WILLIAMS, J. D., *The Compleat Strategyst: Being a Primer on the Theory of Games of Strategy.* New York: McGraw-Hill Book Company, Inc., June 1954.

WOLF, CHARLES, JR., *Foreign Aid: Theory and Practice in Southern Asia.* Princeton, New Jersey: Princeton University Press, June 1960.